ONE MAN'S ENGLAND

ONE MAN'S ENGLAND

W. G. HOSKINS

BRITISH BROADCASTING CORPORATION

Published by the
British Broadcasting Corporation
35 Marylebone High Street
London W1M 4AA

I S B N 0 563 17486 2 (hardback)
I S B N 0 563 17519 2 (paperback)

First published 1978

Printed in England by
Chorley & Pickersgill Ltd, Leeds

Front cover, Wasdale Head in the Lake District. Originally the whole of this bit of country was thickly covered with glacial débris in the form of millions of stones. They were cleared to form the massive walls that formed the boundaries to the small fields. Those stones which were surplus to require- ment for field-walls were neatly piled in roughly circular mounds as we see here.

Back cover (*top*), the author in Ashby Pastures: one of the most famous fox-coverts in the Quorn country of High Leicestershire. Though now wooded, but only lightly, it gets its name from the fact that it originated as a rough piece of ground allotted to the parish of Ashby Folville at the parliamentary enclosure in the late eighteenth century. As it was useless to the villagers as a cow pasture, they rented it to the Quorn who planted it up to give additional cover and breeding-places for the sacred fox.

Back cover (*bottom*), Delph Locks on the Dudley Canal in the Black Country. Originally called Black Delph, the locks (at first nine and now eight) were necessary in order to bring the canal up from the lower ground to the top of the Midland plateau. They were first made in the 1770s and rebuilt as eight locks in 1858. The locks are still in use, as is most of the intricate canal system of the Black Country.

Picture research by Diana Souhami. All the colour illustrations, including those on the cover, and black and white plates 9, 20, 25, 26, 32, 36, 42, 56, 60, 61, 65, 69,81 were taken by Peter Jones who produced the *Landscapes of England* television series, on which this book is based.

Other sources for illustrations are as follows: plate 4 RCHM, 5 Committee for Aerial Photography Cambridge, 10 J. Allan Cash, 12 Committee for Aerial Photography Cambridge, 15 Aerofilms, 16 Leicester University, 21 NBR, 30 James Austin, 31 Edwin Smith, 37 Leicester University, 43 Central Library Oxford, 44 Thomas Photos Oxford, 48 Mavis Batey, 50 Western Morning News Plymouth, 51 Edwin Smith, 62 Bodleian Library, 64 H. M. Parker, 70 Lynn Willies, 77 Aerofilms, 78 Edwin Smith, 79 Forestry Commission, 85 Aerofilms, 86 A. F. Kersting, 98 Frank Booker.

The maps were drawn by Gordon Cramp Studio.

The watercolour of Ivychurch, plate 34, was specially painted for the book by John Piper.

Contents

Acknowledgements

The twelve television programmes represented in this book owe much to numerous collaborators, if that is the right word in this context. The choice of the places to use was my own, hence the title of this book – *One Man's England* – but I owe much to those who turned my ideas into reality. First of all, the producer Peter Jones; then Nat Crosby, whose brilliant camerawork is always beyond criticism, and his assistants Mike Radford, Neil Kennedy, and Rick Stratton; and the sound recordist Simon Wilson who was most patient with someone quite stupid about all things mechanical. The producer's assistants, Sheila Johns and Rita Cooper, made all the practical side work smoothly though one of them refused an order to lay her head on the rails of the main London–Edinburgh line to tell us if she could hear a train coming for the cameraman's benefit. Of the film editors, who work in the back rooms, and do a great deal to produce the finished product, Clare Douglas and Alan Lewens, I saw them at work and entirely failed to understand what they were doing: much too technical for me. Even their language was mysterious. Usually invisible in the sky was Tim Wheeldon, but his helicopter enabled us to get results we could otherwise never have got. There were many others behind the scenes, but I must particularly mention Phil Daly, now Head of Bristol BBC, who finally persuaded me to undertake another six programmes after the success of the first six.

Several local societies helped us to find hidden locations which we could easily have missed, above all the Black Country Society, the Peak Mines Historical Society, and the Wealden Iron Research Group, all invaluable specialists in their own fields. An old friend John Fursdon, of Fursdon in the heart of Devon, went out of his way to find for us (and let us use) a small paddock on his estate where we could have absolute quiet for our recording. Even in the depths of the English countryside, the total peace demanded by the sound recordist is almost never to be found. At Fursdon, a single cirl bunting singing high above us caused the sound recordist to look heavenward and swear at the unnecessary noise it was making in the joy of spring. This tiny bird crept into another programme, however: but a keen critic, a woman ornithologist, later asked me what a cirl bunting was doing singing in February in Dorset, not its natural habitat and not the right time of the year. I could not answer this question, much as I admire total accuracy in work.

Further Reading

The list below is necessarily highly selective, and I am aware that there are some good books I have been obliged to omit for reasons of space.

Armstrong, Patrick, *The Changing Landscape* [*East Anglia*] (Terence Dalton, 1975)

Aston, Michael, and Rowley, Trevor, *Landscape Archaeology* (David & Charles, 1974)

Beresford, Maurice, and Hurst, J. G., *Deserted Medieval Villages* (Lutterworth Press, 1971)

Brandon, Peter, *The Sussex Landscape* (Hodder & Stoughton, 1974)

Brunskill, R. W., *Vernacular Architecture of the Lake Counties* (Faber, 1974)

Clarke, Rainbird, *East Anglia* (Thames & Hudson, 1960)

Ellis, Colin, *Leicestershire and the Quorn Hunt* (Backus, [Leicester] 1951)

Emery, Frank, *The Oxfordshire Landscape* (Hodder & Stoughton, 1974)

Ford, Trevor D. (and others) (ed.), *Lead Mining in the Peak District* (Peak Park Planning Board, 2nd edn 1975)

Gambleson, Robert, *Man in Lakeland* (Dalesman Press, 1975)

Hadfield, Charles, *British Canals* (Phoenix, 1959)

Hoskins, W. G., *The Leicestershire Landscape* (Hodder & Stoughton, 1957)

Hoskins, W. G. (ed.), *History from the Farm* (Faber, 1970)

Hoskins, W. G., *English Landscapes* (BBC, 1973)

Hoskins, W. G., *The Making of the English Landscape* (Hodder & Stoughton, new edn 1977)

Howe, J. Allen, *The Geology of Building Stones* (Edward Arnold, 1910)

Lambert, J. M. (and others), *The Making of the Broads* (R.G.S. Research Series, no. 3, 1960)

Margary, Ivan, *Roman Ways in the Weald* (Phoenix, revised edn 1965)

Millward, R. and Robinson, A., *The South-West Peninsula* (Macmillan, 1971)

Millward, R. and Robinson, A., *The West Midlands* (Macmillan, 1971)

Millward, R. and Robinson, A., *The Lake District* (Eyre & Spottiswoode, 1973)

Millward, R. and Robinson, A., *The Peak District* (Eyre Methuen, 1975)

Munby, L. M. (ed.), *East Anglia Studies* (Heffer, 1968)

Newton, Robert, *The Northumberland Landscape* (Hodder & Stoughton, 1972)

Palliser, David, *The Staffordshire Landscape* (Hodder & Stoughton, 1976)

Piper, John, *Romney Marsh* (Penguin Books, 1950)

Raistrick, Arthur, *The Pennine Dales* (Eyre & Spottiswoode, 1968)

Rowley, Trevor, *The Shropshire Landscape* (Hodder & Stoughton, 1972)

Rowley, Trevor (ed.), *Anglo-Saxon Settlement and Landscape* (British Arch. Reports, no. 6, 1974)

Scarfe, Norman, *The Suffolk Landscape* (Hodder & Stoughton, 1972)

Steane, John, *The Northamptonshire Landscape* (Hodder & Stoughton, 1974)

Taylor, Christopher, *Dorset* (Hodder & Stoughton, 1970)

Taylor, Christopher, *Fields in the English Landscape* (Dent, 1975)

Trueman, A. E., *The Scenery of England and Wales* (Gollancz, 1938)

White, J. T., *The South-East: Down and Weald* (Eyre Methuen, 1977)

Witney, K. P., *The Jutish Forest* [*Kent*] (Athlone Press, 1976)

Wordsworth, William, *Guide to the Lakes* (various editions)

Introduction

This book of twelve essays about different parts of England accompanies the television programmes *Landscapes of England* which were first shown in 1976 and the second series in 1978. They were never intended to cover England systematically but dealt with those parts I knew well and about which I had something to say that was new. Each essay has a theme, sometimes more than one theme, but not one of them aims at covering a whole county or even a 'region', a horrid word that smacks of the lecture hall or the schoolroom.

I have explored England, or parts of it, now for sixty years, for pure pleasure, often not knowing what I was really looking at. It was a long time before it dawned on me that everything I looked at was asking questions: how did it come to be like this? Then I began going to places specially to find the answers, in local documents or on the ground itself.

The book ranges from the Anglo-Scottish Border in the extreme north down to Dorset and its heaths in the south; and from the Broads of eastern England across to the Black Country in the west Midlands. There was a wide range of country to choose from, and the BBC gave me a free hand in choosing. I chose those bits of England I already knew well and which I had studied with a fresh eye, but once or twice I decided to see some special bit of country for myself, for the first time, to give myself a break and to see what I could make of it.

In particular I was fascinated by the way the boundary ran between England and Scotland today, the curious kinks and bulges that suggested a peculiar history, as it obviously had; and I also chose the Black Country, even though it was not an inviting title for a programme, because I had not seen it for some thirty years and had heard that it had been 'cleaned up'. Sadly, this proved to be true: the tortured landscape I remembered from early explorations, the amazing monuments of the early Industrial Revolution like nowhere else, nearly all had gone. It proved to be hard to find a piece of the original landscape amid the high-rise flats, the nondescript buildings in the renovated streets. I tried to remember that it was vastly cleaner than it had been, far better to live in in many ways and too easy to lament the vanished ugliness if one does not have to live in it. Yet it is still a remarkable landscape and I found little pockets (with the aid of good local guides in the Black Country Society) which I felt should be preserved as reminders of an almost vanished history.

Every few square miles of England has its own marked character and there were some I deeply regretted having to leave out of my calculations. I wished above all I could have dwelt a little more on the Isle of Portland, that great limestone rock that Hardy called 'the Gibraltar of the West' – the island (for it was once) which had attracted Mesolithic man seven or eight thousand years ago, an early landfall as they came up the Channel, the island of almost solid limestone of fine quality out of which many famous buildings have been dug, including St Paul's Cathedral: and all the history between – the Romano-British settlements marked on the map of the island, the still-open medieval fields, the Georgian parish church which probably marks the heyday of the vast quarries in the eighteenth century. More than any other small piece of England it appeals to me as a book waiting to be written.

It is even possible to study the landscape of a single parish, and here I was tempted by a remarkable old book, Richard Gough's *History of the Parish of Myddle*, written in the closing years of the seventeenth century and full of detail about the topography of the parish and what men had done to it to change it to a scene so different today, above all the draining of the old meres and creating a landscape of good farmland. Indeed, the meres of Shropshire are another of those peculiar landscapes which I wish I could have had in the programmes.

So the choice of landscapes in this book is not a random one. Not only had it to be bits of England I already knew, except for the odd deviation or two, but also they had to be well scattered about the country – a fair distribution so as to please as many people as possible, though I well know that some will be surprised at not seeing their favourite bit of country analysed and portrayed; but also I had to find some dominant theme in order to show the ingenuity of 'the old men' in adapting themselves to whatever they found underfoot as they penetrated new lands. Sometimes this only dawned on me after wandering round the landscape with the producer and arguing about what we saw. This was particularly true of the Breckland and the Broads, and also of the mills and mines of Derbyshire.

The landscapes, and the fragments thereof, were so widely different that it is almost idle to say what struck me most on the ground, but I think my abiding impressions are of two totally different scenes. One is of the chain-shop in the Black Country, the last chain-shop which makes chains by hand, and chains big enough to work on an oil-rig in the turbulent North Sea, with a handful of men in a Heath Robinson building hammering white-hot iron in pairs with a wonderful mathematical precision, every blow exactly timed to a fraction of a second. And at the other extreme those immense saucers on Goonhilly Downs in Cornwall, searching the firmament for the faintest of signals from space. One the height of scientific sophistication; the other the last of the old hand-made world. These impressions are not an artificial juxtaposition, though they represent two extremes: that is how they stick in my mind. The Black Country boss telling me how his chains of cast iron were better than steel for the oil-rigs; and the neatly dressed engineer at Goonhilly saying in a matter-of-fact voice in one room, 'This is where we cover the Middle East. . . .'

This book is too short for me, but I hope it conveys something about one man's England.

1. Ancient Dorset

There is not just one English landscape, there are probably a hundred or more, and man's making of them has taken very different forms in different parts of England. The process of creating England as we know it, tackling the great wastelands of heath and moor, marshland and forest and mountains, began much farther back in time than we ever thought.

When I was young – and I have spent a lifetime of study since – I felt in my bones that the landscape itself was speaking to me, in a language that I did not understand, and I had to find out how to read it. I used maps, old documents, anything else that historians use, but I am still convinced that the final evidence lies in the reading of the landscape itself, seeing what lies underneath the surface – rather like a surgeon looking at the human body.

Dorset is not only distinctive in its own right, but it has preserved particularly well man's earliest imprint on the landscape because it is essentially a pastoral county and there has been little or no ploughing for centuries. At first sight it has an inhospitable and, in fact, a dangerous coast, nevertheless some of the earliest men to reach this country arrived on the leeward side of Portland Bill some seven or eight thousand years ago. Some of them moved not far inland and did some primitive farming. There is actual evidence that they ate limpets, cockles and winkles brought back from the shore, so they lived, as far as we know, on coastal patches, beginning the colonisation of this huge natural landscape.

Now landscape depends in the end on geology and soils, especially for the earliest farmers with their very crude methods of opening up the soil. They almost certainly bypassed what now seems to be good farmland, because it was so well treed. A good bit of Dorset, in the east anyway, is miles and miles of brown heathland, like Thomas Hardy's famous Egdon Heath. I used to think that this was natural landscape, you got this vegetation – heather, gorse and so on – because the soil is sand and gravel. It all looks untouched, but something extraordinary must have happened because if you look at a map of this part of Dorset the heathlands are scattered pretty thickly with Bronze Age burial mounds. Man was living and dying there thirty to forty centuries ago. The mounds are his burial places but he must have been farming there as well. Indeed traces of Mesolithic man have been found on Winfrith Heath – a mere scratching at the surface that has left no visible traces, but was perhaps the very beginnings of farming.

The soil is terribly thin; it could not have produced much in the way of crops but they were forced to use it because they had not got a heavy enough plough for better soils. The Neolithic men and the men who followed the Bronze Age men cleared the heathlands. That lasted a thousand years or more, but they must have abandoned the great windy cold heaths at some point, probably because the climate deteriorated. Nature rapidly took over again on this kind of soil; man was there a long time, but you would never think so.

One of the earliest visible signs in the landscape is the burial mounds. One, on Oakley Down, is over thirty centuries old. These people made clearings for farming but then, about 3000 years ago, the Iron Age people began to create something which I think was new in the landscape – villages. The site at Woodcutts, a mile from the modern hamlet, started as a single farmstead before the Roman conquest. It has been excavated, and we know that it gradually became a village – hence the rather complex pattern of the site – lasted for a few centuries, and was finally abandoned about AD 370, probably because better land was cleared lower down. Water is scarce indeed up on the hills, so there is a well on this site. It is no less than 136 feet deep. Romano-British farmers dug a well of that tremendous depth to get down to the water-table and the water they needed. The whole landscape of this piece of country, now relatively under-populated, is in fact plastered with Roman sites.

Many of the modern villages, like Sixpenny Handley and Woodyates, are right on top of ancient Romano-British village sites. As a result, a lot of evidence of very early settlement is simply not get-at-able because it lies underneath living villages. Cranborne Chase was a huge area said to be eighty miles around, and in primeval times almost certainly wooded, with some natural clearings. It contains an extraordinary number of settlements, sometimes single farms which are actually on top of sites going back to the Roman age, and even beyond.

Dorset remained very much a native British, or Celtic, part of England. Even before the Roman empire collapsed, the English, the Anglo-Saxons, were raiding, and the people of Dorset were trying to keep them out with great dykes across strategic gaps in the forest. One of the best is Bokerley Dyke. We know that in the year 367 the Anglo-Saxons were putting pressure on the Romans, and it looks as though Bokerley Dyke, a tremendous earthwork, taken over as a county boundary long ago between Dorset and Hampshire, was an attempt to keep out the invading Saxons.

When Bokerley Dyke was eventually overrun, the British put up other ditches, like Comb's Ditch behind it. As a result, the Anglo-Saxons, the old English, arrived later in Dorset than elsewhere in England. But they came into country already being farmed, and imposed on it their own particular pattern. In a remote valley in Purbeck we find the evidence for this where the landscape, despite its first appearance, is in fact basically a planned one. The planning comes through the boundaries, and the boundaries of each estate were regarded as practically sacred. As the Bible itself says, 'Cursed be he that moveth his neighbour's landmark.' The Anglo-Saxon charters often started off with a curse in magnificent language, usually called the 'anathema', saying much the same thing, and that is why the boundaries still survive.

Purbeck country is almost solid stone, but at a perimeter boundary, the boundary of an estate, dense vegetation was allowed to grow up. A blackthorn hedge is pretty impenetrable, and the thicker it is, the denser it is, the older it is; so you get a permanent feature of the landscape.

Wareham, which is completely surrounded by a great earthen bank, was an Anglo-Saxon fortress. The most exciting thing from our point of view is that in one of the churches – St Mary's – survive a number of inscriptions in stone which show that the British lived on here from the seventh to the tenth century and probably longer, despite the English Conquest. History books give the impression that we had a series of conquests – Roman, Saxon, Norman and all the rest and that each one, each lot, slaughtered the existing inhabitants and started a new landscape. This is pure rubbish. The interesting thing about English history is that it goes on continuously. There was not indiscriminate slaughter – unless the natives gave trouble. The British lived on side by side with the Saxons, probably peacefully. Then came the threat from the Danes, a different problem altogether. The Saxons had to make this fortress at Wareham, guarding the whole of this part of the county, the south-east; at the same time they replanned the whole of the street pattern to almost a grid-iron pattern, which we used to think was not used until after the Norman conquest. Done by the Anglo-Saxons, it means that we have a little town with probably a continuous history of occupation since before the Romans, right through the so-called Roman Conquest, right through the Saxon Conquest – and a living town to this day.

Not far from Wareham there is a very remote little stream, the Winterborne, which is a pure English name, meaning the stream that only flows in winter. It attracted a whole string of villages called Winterborne Stickland, Winterborne Tomson – Winterborne everything if you like. Beautiful Dorset names. Winterborne Tomson church, built in the 1100s, was one of Thomas Hardy's favourite churches. It is a perfect example of a twelfth-century parish church on a small scale, and it has a beautiful little Georgian interior. The village itself has gone. Several of the Winterbornes are today just humps in a field.

As the villages grew in size, populations grew, and they were compelled to take over land that they had previously used for ordinary pasture, to take it over for growing essential crops. But Dorset is also a countryside of extremely steep hills, and at Worth Matravers they created artificial cultivation terraces up the side of the hill, wider terraces that followed the contours. So all over the Dorset map you find these so-called 'lynchets'.

Everything is more ancient than it looks, and than we think. But that does not mean that it remains static. At Abbotsbury we have one of the major new directions in landscape history with the foundation of a great Benedictine abbey in King Canute's reign. Abbeys all over England made their own big imprint on the landscape. The most conspicuous thing at Abbotsbury is the enormous tithe barn, fifteenth-century and too big for any modern farmer. The abbey collected the tithes into this huge place, the monks taking a tenth of everything, even to the feathers off the breast of the geese. You can imagine the feeling against the monks, but the peasantry had to put up with it.

One of the special features of monastic landscapes was the creation of big fishponds. Even in a monastery as near the sea as Abbotsbury they could not rely upon the sea for the regular supply of fish they needed, so out of a tiny stream they created a very big fishpond for the supply of the abbey.

Then, on top of the neighbouring hill, the abbey built a lovely little chapel in the fourteenth century dedicated to St Catherine, as a landmark for sailors out at sea. This was one of the side contributions of abbeys near the coast.

The monks of Abbotsbury lasted for 500 years. Their civilisation ended abruptly in the reign of Henry VIII, but all around I can see traces of what they have left behind, and layers of older history, going right back – as it does all over Dorset – through the old English, the Roman, the prehistoric. It is still there, the ancient landscape.

1

2

1. Winfrith Heath is one of a chain of heaths in south-east Dorset, mostly covered with gorse and heathers now, but once cultivated. Numerous Bronze Age barrows testify to former habitation, and indeed on Winfrith Heath traces of mesolithic man (*c.* 8000–6000 BC) have been found with minute evidence that seems to suggest early scrapings at the soil, the beginnings of farming. Winfrith Heath is commonly supposed to be the famous Egdon Heath of *The Return of the Native*, but Hardy made it clear that it embodied at least a dozen heaths in this region and not just one. An Atomic Energy Station is built on the heath. One wonders what Hardy would have made of this twentieth-century monster.

2. 'Strip lynchets' at Worth Matravers in the Isle of Purbeck. These steep contours in a countryside of rising population compelled medieval farmers to level out the hillside in terraces in order to make more land accessible for farming. They are to be found in many parts of England in similar locations and their precise antiquity is still a matter for archaeological debate.

3. The tithe barn at Abbotsbury is one of the largest in the country. Even in its truncated form (at one end) it is no less than 276 feet long. Here the abbey gathered in the tithes of all the lands over which it had rights. It is a magnificent piece of fifteenth-century building.

4. Wareham is a remarkable example of a planned town, probably laid out before the Norman Conquest. It is, however, much older than this as a town. Several memorial inscriptions in St Mary's Church at Wareham show that the British remained here in force as late as the seventh to ninth centuries, and there is no reason to doubt that the town has been continuously occupied since well back in Roman times. The Saxon ramparts are still abundantly clear.

5. Unlike Woodcutts, which stands firmly above ground and is a prominent feature of the local scene (plate 7), Turnworth shows up best from the air, with its pattern of Iron Age fields and a circular ditched enclosure which represents a contemporary farmstead. Though the site was deserted for a time, it was taken over for ploughing in medieval times and later. The prehistoric pattern is, however, clear, even to the narrow track that winds through it.

6

7

6. Small villages lined the banks of the Winterborne stream, some of which have disappeared. Such streams occur elsewhere, meaning a stream which only flows in chalk country when the water-table rises in winter. At Winterborne Tomson the village itself has vanished (traces can be detected in the field near the church), but the perfect little parish church remains – a rare survival of a twelfth-century parish church which retains its Norman apse. It was restored beautifully by A. R. Powys with the aid of money from the sale of one of Thomas Hardy's manuscripts – Hardy loved this church. The harmonium at the west end may well be the one he heard so long ago.

7. Woodcutts lies all alone, a perfect example of a Romano-British settlement. It was first occupied before the Roman Conquest as a single farmstead, gradually growing with a succession of wooden huts into a small village, and finally abandoned about AD 370.

8. Portland is a solid mass of limestone, broken at the edges by the sea and inland by extensive quarrying over the centuries. In sheltered hollows on the leeward side of the island (the eastern side) traces have been found of mesolithic occupation by people who collected limpets and other small seafood at the tideline and carried them up to their habitation site about 200 feet above the shore. As a site, it contrasts with the inland site at Winfrith (plate 1) where there is some slight evidence of farming by scratching the soil for poor, thin crops.

9

10

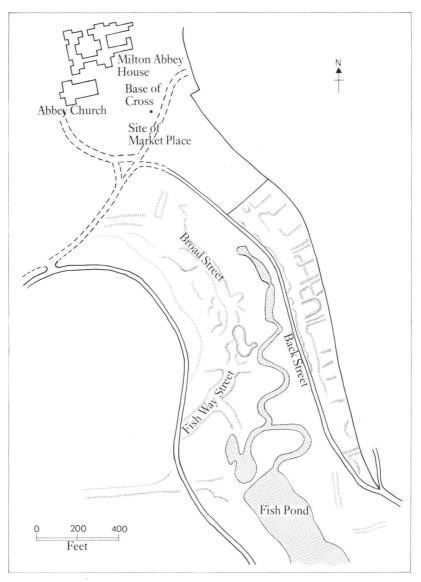

9. Cranborne Chase was once densely wooded. With the clearance of much of the forest it became a hunting-chase and was used for this purpose by several kings.

10. The Vale of Marshwood is quite unlike any other part of Dorset to look at. Unlike the chalk downlands it is still densely wooded and closely resembles east Devon with its high hedgebanks, small fields and dispersed farmsteads. Mostly a medieval landscape, though the Saxons and possibly the Romano-British were clearing the woodland before that.

11. Plan of the deserted market-town of Milton Abbas, as excavated. In 1786 Joseph Damer swept it away in order to enlarge the park of his new mansion, and rebuilt the 'model village' some distance along the road. The park and the new village are well worth seeing.

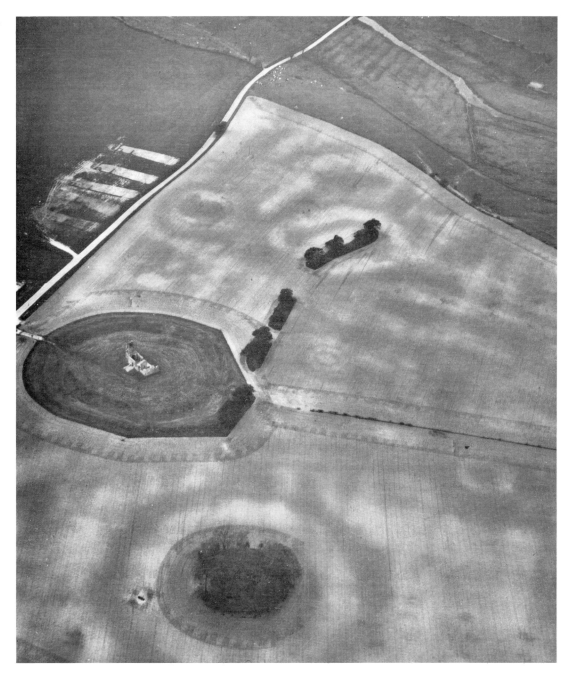

12. Knowlton church (now in ruins) lies in the centre of a large encircling bank and ditch dating in all probability from a Bronze Age site of worship. Clearly this was a Christian take-over of a long-used pagan site, as at Brent Tor (plate 100) but here the evidence is much more obvious.

2. The Lake District: The Conquest of the Mountains

I cannot think of a better description of this piece of England than an eloquent little passage from Wordsworth's *Guide to the Lakes*. Envisaging someone looking at the natural landscape before man had appeared on the scene, he says: '. . . he will form to himself an image of the tides visiting and revisiting the friths . . . the rivers pursuing their course to be lost in the mighty mass of waters. He may see or hear in fancy the winds sweeping over the lakes, or piping with a loud voice among the mountain peaks; and, lastly, may think of the primeval woods shedding and renewing their leaves with no human eye to notice, or human heart to regret or welcome the change.'

This piece of mountain country looks as if it is the work entirely of Nature in its most volcanic mood, and yet it is quite deceptive. These mountains were wooded up to the summits, over 2000 feet, and the woodland was cleared by prehistoric man with a stone axe of a kind which has been found up on the Pike of Stickle. There was a tremendous trade in these axes; they have been found in Dorset, Wiltshire and Hampshire, and we call the places where they were made 'axe factories'. The men of that time discovered in this great mass of rock an intrusive rock harder than all the rest. How they found it we do not know.

The Lake District, shaped and formed to a great extent during the last Ice Age, has seen numerous vegetational changes since the retreat of the glaciers. The whole landscape was scoured of vegetation, but the ice left behind enough surface soil for the high country to be recolonised: in other words, for the trees to come back. We know all this from identifying the pollen from trees found in the sediments of the lakes. We know exactly what sorts of trees grew, and at what height. By Neolithic times, say 4000 to 5000 years ago, the mountains were wooded, and man was beginning to clear the forest from above.

But it was not only primitive man working with his axes and, probably, with fire, who opened up this landscape, creating clearings for his animals. The animals helped him; the sheep and goats, above all, munched every seedling tree that tried to grow again. Not much is left of the original woodland. Botanists, however, recognise what they call 'relict' woodland, patches of what the mountain fells must have looked like originally. Miles of what are now bare fells were once heavily wooded.

Since the prehistoric axe trade developed very early on, you find ancient trade routes, now mere mountain tracks, most of them, crossing the high passes. There is one track called

High Street, not in the sense that we use it in modern towns, since the emphasis is on *High* and it runs to 1700 feet. These tracks have been in use since prehistoric times, and the modern fell walker still uses them. Near one of the 'axe factories', an axe was picked up which had been trodden on by fell walkers and scratched by them for years before anybody realised what it really was.

The Romans had no reason to interfere with the natives in the remote hills and dales, provided they gave no trouble, and thus they have left very little imprint. Life went on at the farming level, but the next enemies came from across the sea, which can be seen gleaming on the horizon from Hard Knott. They came from the West, from Ireland, though in fact they were Norwegians. First they came to plunder, then they settled and became colonists. They not only took over the old settlements, they were also the first people to push into the heart of the mountains, up the dales, to create new ones. Their imprint on the landscape, though exaggerated, I think, by the number of names of Norse origin, was very powerful indeed.

The name Watendlath is pure Scandinavian, meaning 'the end of the water', which is a quite characteristic setting in the Lake District. Three or four farmsteads grouped together, for security probably, and co-operation in farming and warmth. It is a hamlet rather than a village. The hamlet kind of settlement is really suited to a pastoral economy with a few cows and sheep on each farm, and probably, coming from Norway with a very similar topography, the Norsemen brought the hamlet with them. It could not expand into a village in such surroundings, when the countryside would support only a limited population no matter what was done to it. 'Thwaite' is the old Norse word for 'clearing'; in some places, the ground was so covered with glacial boulders that it gave its name to the whole settlement – hence, Stonethwaite. You get a very good idea of the primeval landscape from the great rock outcrops which show what kind of country the Norse colonists had to tackle.

Wast Water is the most sinister of the lakes. It is the deepest, the darkest and on the east side the mountain tumbles into it in screes on a slope of about one in two. No man could touch this, it is just as Nature left it.

But on the other side of the lake there was an extraordinary population of farmers in the sixteenth century. Forty farmers down one side, another sixteen or so at the top, at Wasdale Head, farming the only flat bits of land in the whole area. A delta is formed by glacial streams coming down from the mountains, and the whole of this flat land is now cultivated for pasture, but was once covered with millions of tons of stone. All these stones had to be picked off the land. They were used for boundary walls mostly, great walls of the kind to be found all round here.

It was not only farming that brought people to the Lake District. The great feudal family, the Percys, who were the power in the north of England, needed a multitude of tenants who could, when necessary, perform military service. The Percys envisaged their tenants not simply as farmers but as potential soldiers in what was virtually their private army.

An enormous area of the fells passed into the ownership of the monasteries. There were about a dozen monasteries around the Lake District of local foundation, with enormous estates, but monasteries as far away as Fountains in Yorkshire also had very big estates here. Their particular contribution to the landscape was the creation of huge green sheep pastures on the fells, for mile after mile. The very big stone-walled pounds are a relic of the monastic sheepfolds. The sheep were gathered in off the open mountains to be either sheared or sold off at the nearest market.

One of the things that impresses me about the Lake District, especially high up, is the poverty in the buildings, the farmhouses and the churches. They were, in a way, poverty-stricken. Although this was a potentially rich countryside, with great sheep pastures, it was owned by other people. The money, the great profits, were drained off and the community was left with the remains. Hence the small poor churches, built with its own money and nobody else's.

A very attractive minor feature of the landscape is the primitive-looking bowed bridge, a single arch over a small stream. One of the best is at Throstlegarth. 'Throstle' means a thrush, 'garth' is the Scandinavian word for an enclosure, and there the sheep were brought in from over the fells and driven to the nearest market.

You could say that landscape history is almost a history of the clearance of natural woodlands; anyway, it is the most important thing. And the development of a new industry making use of timber can have a profound influence in this process. And sometimes the whole social history of an area comes into the story.

In the sixteenth century, Queen Elizabeth's time, the rich minerals of this district were found, probably for the first time. Elizabeth brought over a number of German experts, top men, and also a lot of miners. They arrived in the Keswick area, but encountering the English hatred of foreigners, the poor old German miners took refuge on one of the islands of Derwent Water, and there they lived for a time. Local feeling eventually died down, and the parish registers show that men with German names were marrying English girls: the German miners were accepted in the local community. The physical effect of mining was an enormous destruction of the woodlands for the smelting of the mineral ores.

In the sixteenth and seventeenth centuries, the yeomen, called the 'statesmen' – which really means the 'estates men', men who own a bit of land – were pushed up into remote dales, such as Martindale, by the increasing pressure of population growth. Their farms are all over the dales, and very high up. Because of the remoteness and the amount of stone – it is really solid rock country – they built their houses of the stones picked off the ground. These stones are unshaped, rough slate, and there is not a speck of mortar in the dry-stone walling. The main reason it stands up is the enormous cornerstones which hold together the four walls of this kind of unmortared masonry.

But even while Wordsworth was eulogising the statesmen in his *Guide to the Lake District*, they were, in fact, a dying race, because of the increasing concentration of land ownership. At Martindale, there is just one statesman's house left. I have no doubt that Martindale was once a hamlet, typical all over the Lake District. They were small farmers earning a hard living; family and animals occupied the same long building. They could not stand years of depression and they slowly went under, but the big men of course *could* stand it and they bought up the small ones: the old English story. The statesmen have gone but their houses remain, distinctive in the landscape.

It was not always possible to make a living off farming alone, and in the village of Hartsop is a very nice example of a dual economy. A very special kind of house, with a gallery in front, it is early seventeenth-century, a type of house you get very much in the north and north-west of England. The ladies of the house came out on to the gallery in the warmer weather to spin their wool. While the farmer was working in the fields, the women and children were doing the spinning. So the landscape of the Lake District, despite first appearances, is really a man-made landscape over 4000 to 5000 years. Woodlands have been cleared, replanted, destroyed again by mining and replanted again, right down to the present day. Two hundred generations of men and women have toiled in their various ways to create this landscape, so magnificent and still so deceptive.

13. Pike of Stickle: over 2000 feet up in 1947 an 'axe factory' was accidentally discovered where Neolithic Man had found a very hard rock which he could fashion into axes that were eventually exported to the far south of England. High up on the face of these tremendous slopes was also found a tiny man-made cave – the 'factory' – only seven feet in depth and five feet at the entrance. Here these axes were fashioned some 4000 years ago. Several other sites have since been found in the hard core of the mountains.

14. Martindale Forest in the remote dale of that name, once a huge natural forest and still retaining large tracts of natural woodland.

28   *The Lake District: The Conquest of the Mountains*

15. Wast Water: the grimmest of the lakes, with a remarkable contrast between one side and the other – the eastern side always quite uncolonised because of its impossible slope and stony screes, the western side more amenable to early farmers and once – above all in the sixteenth century – thickly dotted with small farms, the tenants of the great feudal family of the Percys.

16. Throstlegarth: a remote sheepfold with a typical packhorse bridge as at Watendlath, though probably for driving the sheep rather than packhorses, as it ends here.

17

18

The Lake District: The Conquest of the Mountains

17. Dale Head: a 'statesman's' house erected at the very frontier of cultivation in a dale off Ullswater. A date-stone shows it was built (or possibly rebuilt) in 1666.

18. Watendlath: here the Norse colonists came to a stop in the face of the mountains ahead. A neat little hamlet based on cattle and sheep farming.

19. Lower Hartsop: a picturesque hamlet of scattered farmhouses and cottages. Spinning wool was the usual by-occupation for the women and children. Many of the bigger houses had a little first-floor gallery which ran the length of the house. It epitomises the dual economy of this harsh country just as the miners-cum-farmers did in the uplands of Derbyshire.

20. Hard Knott Fort, at the head of Eskdale, commanding a view right down to the sea. From here the Romans could control the natives below. They had no interest in colonising this difficult country themselves so long as the natives kept quiet.

3. North Norfolk:
Marsh and Sea

Along the marshland coast of north Norfolk lie a score of silted-up and mostly deserted harbours and ports that flourished from 100 to 500 years ago. The mud glistens where ships once rode, or there may even be grassland with no trace at all of the former body of water. It is a cold and, humanly speaking, a lonely coast. Therein lies most of its distinctive charm.

But back from the sea ancient churches speak of former glory. Norfolk once had no fewer than 900 churches, one to every three square miles. Churches do not simply stand on the ground; they belong to the landscape, are part of it as much as an ancient hedge or an old woodland, growing out of it like the corn and the grass, and built of the stone of the very soil. This is a county famous for grand churches, bigger than any congregation a small village could ever have produced. Such churches were built for the greater glory of God, and were not limited by their need of only a few hundred seats.

The church at Salthouse is superb. Even when empty, it is so atmospheric that it talks to me and, in its own way, reveals the former prosperity of the community. Inscriptions in the shiny black paving describe some Salthouse men as merchants. On the choir stalls, Elizabethan schoolboys have left their own particular graffiti – sailing-ships. There is little doubt that in the sixteenth century the church, or the chancel anyway, became the village school during the week, where boys were taught the three essentials – reading, writing and, above all, the art of navigation.

Incidentally, 'Salthouse' is one place name which means what it says. In the eleventh century it was the site of a salt warehouse, a collecting depot for salt made all around the Wash and along the coast. Salt was a most valuable commodity.

One of the very noticeable things about the Norfolk landscape is the number of ruined churches, like the gaunt and melancholy church at Egmere, out of use probably since Henry VIII's time. There are well over a hundred such churches; I think there are probably more ruined churches in Norfolk than in the rest of England put together. Egmere Church was the centre of a once-flourishing village which decayed in the fifteenth century owing to loss of population, mainly through plague, and became too poor to support the priest. The church was neglected; in Henry VIII's time the squire did the classic thing – took the lead off the roof because it was valuable even then. Of course, it is the quickest way to finish any building off, and the church is reported as in decay in Queen Elizabeth's reign.

An extraordinary number of Norfolk churches are quite isolated. Not as we used to think because the village has gone and the church has stayed: in certain places, there is no evidence of a village. Edingthorpe is one example; there are others all over Norfolk. And at Holkham, the church stands all by itself, but here we know why. The old village, quite close to the church, was completely demolished by Thomas Coke, Earl of Leicester, in 1734, in order to build his great house. The village stood in the way of his plans, and he rebuilt it down on the main road, outside his park. This happened, of course, in other parts of England where great landlords had absolute control.

Holkham itself is a masterpiece of architecture by William Kent, begun in 1734, finished in 1761. The park, nine miles around, is a typical great English park. Capability Brown, the greatest of English landscape gardeners, created the terraced gardens nearer the house, also the beautiful lake, and completed the whole scheme in 1762. The Cokes of Holkham, that is to say the Earls of Leicester – who incidentally have nothing to do with Leicester – at the height of their wealth owned 44,000 acres in Norfolk. Thomas Coke, besides creating a great house, park and landscaped gardens, was reorganising his farms over that enormous estate, creating a new piece of the English landscape. The Cokes represented a new attitude of mind; they introduced new techniques of farming, especially on light soils. They began to exploit their estates commercially in a big way in the eighteenth century, in a businesslike way that represented a revolution in English agriculture. Such great men were the principal agents in changing the landscape.

At Holkham, a marvellous landscape was created by a great landlord; from the middle of Salthouse marshes, almost everything you see is a landscape created by the peasants. The rules which governed the making of this bleak-looking landscape on the marshes were simply those of making a living. Every community is presented with a unique set of problems in its use of the land, and the village of Salthouse was no exception. The villagers found themselves in surroundings which placed very great limits on their choice of arable and good pasture.

The parish itself, and the village, is dominated by a rough heath rising to about 300 feet above the sea. I am told that it is the result of the ice sheet of the last Ice Age retreating to the north and leaving behind this high heathland of débris, which is basically sand and gravel, and thus creating this marvellous, but very infertile, heath country.

The peasants of Salthouse could not grow any crops up there. The heath formed a huge barrier, and the village fields could not be extended in that direction. Under the heath is a very narrow belt of arable land which is above any flood level and obviously chosen specially for that reason. Below the arable is the village itself, which comes to an end equally abruptly at the present main road. This was another old frontier. The sea once came right up to it. Beyond was the marshland, flowed over by every tide, and reclaimed from the sea at different periods. You can see the enormous extent of it along this coastland.

On the Salthouse marshes, and probably on all the others in this part of Norfolk, the reclamation of the land was done partly by banking, and partly by digging great channels. After about a year or so, with rain washing out the salt content, cattle and sheep can be brought on to the marsh, and that is the beginning of new farmland.

There is still a huge expanse of salt marsh awaiting reclamation, thousands of acres all along the coast and around the Wash. It is easy to see the difference between the rich green pastures of the fresh marsh and the rather more barren salt marsh. In fact, man is only completing a process that Nature had long ago begun. Salt marshes only develop in sheltered places, high up estuaries, or behind shingle bars, as sand or mud flats, exposed at low tide. These silt banks provide a hold for vegetation, and this causes an even greater deposition of mud by obstructing the flow of water. So the silt builds up until, eventually, only the highest tides cover the marsh. And then man enters the scene to keep all the tides out.

Inevitably, this work attracted the big landlords with the capital to do things in a grand way. The whole of the marshland is honeycombed with little creeks and watercourses. At dead low-water, it looks very harmless. The great seabank at Morston winds for miles. Parts of it were made in 1793, and the whole job – there is so much of it – took about thirty years. It was the time of the Napoleonic Wars and high corn prices, and I imagine that only great landlords, like the Earls of Leicester at Holkham, could possibly have reclaimed land on this huge scale.

On this little bit of coast, described as the finest example of coastal marshes in these islands, are an extraordinary number of places, sometimes partly decayed, that were in fact once thriving little ports. This coast buzzed with sailing-ships of twenty to thirty or forty tons. That may not sound very much, but modern lorries of the same capacity thunder through tiny English villages. These ships were the lorry traffic of the time. It was a great coast for sending out corn, and bringing back coal; Overy Staithe was used up to 1914 for bringing in coal.

A couple of miles inland, on the banks of the little river Glaven, is the village of Cley, once a seaport and a fishing village. The splendid church, overlooking a green that was once a busy port, is now isolated. We know from a map of 1586 that most of the village then lay round the church. So why did it move? I think that the seabanks that took in the salt marshes for pasture obstructed the river channels up to Cley. But, despite the opposition of the locals to the destruction of their coastal and fishing trades, the Cley Marsh continued to be embanked and reclaimed until about 1650. And as the tide was pushed farther back, so to speak, the settlement at Cley simply kept moving nearer the sea until eventually they gave up altogether. The present village is at least a mile short of the deep channel.

There was a great deal more traffic on the roads and the little rivers of medieval England than we think. The earliest crossings of the rivers were by fords; and on the river Glaven is a place called Glandford, which means Glaven Ford. This was immediately above the tidal limit, and is described in the thirteenth century as the 'King's Highway'. There are times when the ford becomes dangerous, so two miles downstream from Glandford, Wiveton Bridge was built. The present bridge is probably fifteenth-century, and has taken the traffic away from the old ford.

If you look at an old road like the A149 as it is today, it winds in a most curious way; it is not a matter of contours at all. I am quite sure that if you ask yourself how our roads originated, you can start off with a cattle track. The cattle on this coastland are still driven to and from the marshes every day. But cattle do not walk in straight lines, they mooch from side to side, eating as they go, and they trample out a path which naturally human beings follow. So the cattle track became a small medieval roadway from village to marsh and eventually village to village.

Above all, on this soft coastline, there has been an incessant battle between land and sea. There are cottages in Salthouse that show the effects of the great flood of 1953, just as the cottages must have done after the medieval flood of 1287, both remembered in the local annals. Man may win huge tracts of marsh from the sea, but from time to time man-made defences break down, and the sea takes a terrible revenge.

21. Coast erosion on the north-east coast of Norfolk. This is all that remains of the parish church of Eccles: the stump of the tower. The village itself has completely gone, except for fragments of roofing-tiles which can be picked up on the beach at low tide.

22. Salthouse: the magnificent parish church stands well above the highest floods. In 1953 a 'sea-surge' broke through the shingle bank and the North Sea poured in to a depth of several feet across the marshes (mid-picture). Much of the village was destroyed, and the church became a vast storehouse for the rescued furniture. The view is taken from the edge of the heathland, looking down over the arable to the marshes.

23. Edingthorpe: the lonely church in the fields of north-east Norfolk. The round western tower is common in Norfolk, usually built of flint which was assumed to be the reason for this unusual design, because flint is almost unworkable; but Pevsner believes that the style came in from the Continent. Of nearly 180 round towers in England, Norfolk has 119 and Suffolk 41. Most are Norman but about a score can be dated as Anglo-Saxon. This is a very characteristic Norfolk country scene.

24. Holkham Hall: the grandest house in Norfolk, built for the Earl of Leicester from 1734 to 1761. The park is immense in size, the landscaped gardens by Capability Brown. At the height of the family fortunes they owned some 44,000 acres, all in Norfolk, and were able to manipulate a whole landscape in all their farms.

25. Overy Staithe: one of the many deserted coastal ports on the north coast of Norfolk. It was not only silting-up that killed this little port (which was working well within living memory) but also the increasing size of ships. Several of these 'lost ports' can be found along this beautiful coast, Thornham being one of the best. 'Staithe' means 'landing-place.'

26. Egmere: one of the loneliest places in mid-Norfolk, a land of wide open spaces and magnificent skies. Behind the church, already in ruins in the time of Elizabeth I, can be discerned the irregularities in the grass which denote where the village once stood. Egmere perished as a church because the village decayed in the interest of sheep-farming, but there are many deeply isolated churches in the countryside which cannot be explained in this way. They never had a village and remain one of the many unsolved problems of the English landscape.

4. Kent: Landscapes of War and Peace

Kent is one of the richest counties in England, and you can see this in the wealth of the medieval farmhouses: an extraordinary number have survived the ravages of time. For centuries, in addition to land put aside for pasture and corn, farmers in Kent used their land for crops that could be sold for cash. When hops were introduced by Flemish immigrants in the sixteenth century, most of the crops then being grown were for consumption by the farmer and his family – subsistence farming.

The typical Kentish yeoman's farm was surrounded by enclosures of 200 acres or so, in which the farmer could introduce new methods and new crops as he pleased. Some farms probably started as a clearing in the woods and developed slowly into villages and even towns, hence the recurrence of 'den' – meaning 'pasture' – as the ending of Kentish place-names. Tenterden started as a clearing in the woodlands for pasturing swine belonging to the men of Thanet, thirty miles away, and developed eventually into a prosperous town with a wide market street. The High Street originated along the drove-road from Thanet to the wooded pastures of the Weald and probably dates from prehistoric times. Its later wealth came from the wool and woollen cloth industry at a time when any industry had to be sited where its raw materials were to hand. When you look at Romney Marsh and the nearby Walland Marsh, you still see tens of thousands of fat sheep. It is one of the great sights of England, a landscape of peace.

The marshes themselves are the result of centuries of reclamation. The Romans started the process by building the immense embankment called the Rhee Wall. This now carries a road, and aims at the coastline, not running *along* it, as you would expect an embankment to do. There has been quite a lot of speculation about this, and about the whole evolution of the marshes. Miles back from the sea, you can still make out the rising slopes of an old coastline. At one time the high tides flowed right up to it, forming a huge lagoon. Behind the shingle ridge, marshes formed on each side of the River Rother. The Rhee Wall was the key to reclaiming the most northerly marshes; and to the south reclamation can be dated as far back as 774. Then, in 1287, a huge sea-storm diverted the Rother and made feasible the final work of reclamation. Parts of the marsh were taken in piecemeal at various dates right down to the sixteenth century.

Between the winding ditches there is a great depth of five feet or so of rich alluvial soil, which makes these marshes some of the most fertile pastures in the country. Farmers here can get ten or twelve sheep to the acre on them all the year round, and on special fields – the 'fattening fields' – up to twenty-five sheep to the acre. Farmers in Australia get about one sheep to every ten acres.

Romney Marsh is one of the richest bits of England and evidence of this richness can be seen in the fine church, which was called Ivychurch even in 1086. It must have been so old then that it was trailing ivy. The present church dates from 1370, and the ivy went long ago, but it means that a church was there in Saxon times. It was built by a monastery at Canterbury which owned most of this rich land. But why build a church like this, and like a dozen others, in what is apparently an unpopulated countryside? We do not know the answer. There must have been people, but 'the sheep have devoured the men'.

From this region English wool was sent abroad where it was highly valued. But in the fourteenth century, little places like Cranbrook attracted hundreds of skilled workers from Flanders, who settled there and began a cloth 'industry'. A splendid 'clother's house' still stands. The part with big windows, and very richly timbered, is the merchant's house; attached to it, across an entrance to the yard, is the workshop end, still attractive, but with very much less timber. It was built for utility, to house the looms; the other was built for ostentatious living, and the quantity of timber incorporated into the buildings was a visible badge of status and wealth.

The Kentish cloth industry used up a great deal of timber, mostly from the Weald, that great stretch of countryside from west Kent right across the middle of Sussex, still one of the most heavily wooded parts of England. But often, in the depths of secluded and isolated clearings, one finds evidence of an industry that seems totally out of place in such a rural piece of countryside. For instance, in the middle of the Weald what looks like a very ordinary field is, in fact, a Roman iron-working site. The farmer himself first noticed three big brown rings in the field, and when he started ploughing, he turned up masses of cinders and slag. He had found a Roman iron-smelting site. The ore was close by; it is picked up in all the fields round about, especially, of course, when they have been ploughed. There is even more impressive evidence to be seen, I think, in the great lumps of waste from the elementary bloomery, a clay furnace, powered by hand bellows, in which a mixture of charcoal and iron ore was smelted to produce a lump of impure iron, not fully molten, that settled at the base of the furnace. The tons of cinders and slag also produced were dumped in the streams. It was the Romans who opened up this almost impenetrable forest in order to get the iron out, but after their disappearance the industry dwindled and the Weald closed up again except for the old drove roads.

What helped to change all that was water power, the discovery that in the working and casting of iron the water-wheel, driving hammers and bellows, could enormously increase output. The large and almost natural-looking ponds scattered throughout the Weald are evidence of this. They are still known as 'hammer' ponds, or, like the one near Cowden, 'furnace' ponds.

The power of water had to be harnessed for the new blast furnaces. Flowing on through a string of ponds, it turned a wheel which pumped the bellows and created heat. The opportunity for developing the industry was in the coming of Henry VIII. He spent most of his reign at war. He had to import his big armaments like cannon until a domestic industry was established. So this piece of country, now deserted and taken over by nature, is really the remains of an armament industry. There is but little visible evidence, just masses of old cinders and slag underlying acres of the green fields.

The effects on the landscape were quite spectacular. Previously, the iron industry had affected only patches, like the little mine-pits where the ore was dug out; these are now mostly lost in the woods and filled with rather stagnant water. But the large-scale use of water power did involve considerable problems, and made a bigger impact. The streams in the Weald are small, so it was not always a matter of constructing a single dam at the bottom end of a valley. On the Sussex side of the Weald is a whole chain of about eleven ponds, which used to feed one big furnace, thus creating a series of reservoirs of water, which would last right through the summer, so that industry did not stop for lack of power in a dry season.

The discovery, in the early eighteenth century, that the use of coal, which was not available in the Weald, was a more efficient method of smelting iron, led to the ultimate downfall of the Kent and Sussex iron industry. In the valley of the little River Teise, near Lamberhurst, fallen masonry marks the site of an old sluice gate, and the start of a long cutting, now blocked by soil. Downstream is the further evidence of slag and furnace waste. The now derelict corn-mill, called Furnace Mill, is almost certainly the site of the old furnace. All that remains of its wheel is a wooden stump set in a rusty iron bearing. When the works finally closed down in 1765, a corn miller took over the old workings. Once you have a source of power you never let it go. Mills go on, although their product may change. Nowadays, the whole valley has been transformed again; the oast-houses of Hoathly Farm dominate the scene.

About a mile further upstream, we come across the site of a big abbey of the Premonstratensian order. The monks of this order, like the Cistercians, loved solitude and remoteness. They came in the early 1200s, and made a clearing and opened up the countryside, and left some superb ruins, which I would call the Fountains Abbey of the South. Bayham Abbey existed for over 300 years, until the time of Henry VIII. It, and all its properties, then passed into lay hands. In this case, mainly to the great Gresham family, rich city merchants who exploited something which the abbey had never bothered about, or perhaps never knew about – the iron ore in the surrounding woods.

The little ponds on the Weald have been likened to a string of beads under the greenwood trees, and these are what one chiefly sees as evidence of a lost industrial landscape. Kipling, who lived in these parts, puts it very well, in Puck's Song:

And mark you where the ivy clings
To Bayham's mouldering walls?
O there we cast the stout railings
That stand around St Paul's.

See you the dimpled track that runs
All hollow through the wheat?
O that was where they hauled the guns
That smote King Philip's fleet.

(Out of the Weald, the secret Weald,
Men sent in ancient years
The horse-shoes red at Flodden Field,
The arrows at Poitiers!)

The landscape of war has reverted to a landscape of peace, as peaceful and as rural as the fat sheep browsing over the Romney Marshes under the summer sun.

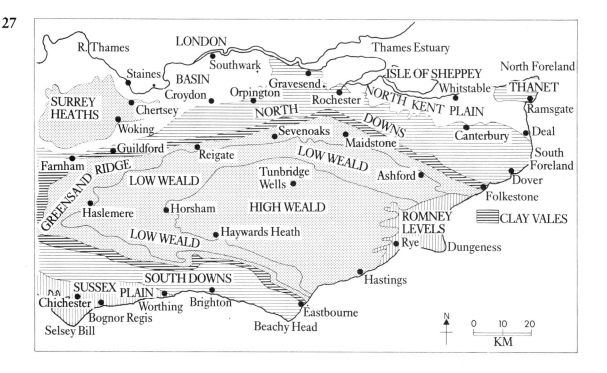

27. The Weald: the map shows something of the original extent of the Weald, which derived its ancient name from the Germanic word *wald* meaning simply 'woodland'. Although largely dismissed by geographers and historians as impenetrable forest, it was in fact traversed by numerous minor Roman roads in the search for iron ore. Indeed, some of these Roman ways may have followed the lines of even older drove-roads along which the villagers in the lowlands drove their pigs in search of acorns (*pannage*). Even so most of the Weald, both in Kent and Sussex, has remained densely wooded, and on the heavy clays nearly impassable for much of the year. Probably in earliest times it stretched unbroken from the Surrey and Hampshire border to the edge of Romney Marshes, except for the coastal levels. The High Weald rises to some 500 feet above sea-level.

The topography and landscape history of the Weald is complicated and has been best studied in a recent book by K. P. Witney, *The Jutish Forest* (1976).

28. Cowden: the furnace pond deep in the Weald where the water was collected before being released to supply the power that was needed for the furnace.

29. The furnace mill near Bayham Abbey: very little of the old iron-working mill is left. It closed down in 1765 and was taken over as a corn-mill. Power was too useful to waste, and many mills in England have passed through various uses for this reason.

30. Kentish medieval farmhouse: Headcorn Manor. Kent had become one of the richest counties in England and its landscape is scattered with large farmhouses dating from the fifteenth and sixteenth centuries, some even earlier.

31. Tenterden: the wide High Street, the kind of street found in all places where large sheep and cattle markets were the source of the local economy, as, say, at Thame in Oxfordshire. But long before it was a main street it had been a drove-road for taking the sheep into the Romney Marshes all the way from Thanet. Or it may have been pigs earlier on, to feed on the acorns of the forest.

32. Bayham Abbey on the borders of Kent and Sussex, founded in the depths of the Weald in the early 1200s. The monks, however, never seem to have recognised the wealth of iron ore all around it in the woods, but their successors – the great predators of the monasteries under Henry VIII – were quick to develop a capitalist industry for the armament trade.

33. Ivychurch: sheep grazing in the churchyard. Romney Marsh, with its fattening pastures for tens of thousands of sheep, wasted no space.

34. Ivychurch: watercolour drawing by John Piper. A large church in the Marsh. Mentioned in the eleventh century as already strung with ivy, so how much older was it even then? The present church is a fine later medieval building, but why these huge churches and so few people unless the sheep had already ousted people even at that early date?

5. The Black Country

It is a tortured and tormented landscape, a bit of south Staffordshire which, because it was rich in coal, iron, and certain kinds of building stones and clays, has been robbed of its resources for centuries and reduced to its present state. When I was there twenty-five years ago it seemed a dreadful piece of countryside, truly a black country, though I appreciated it even then. But it is a landscape which is being remade with the enormous energy which the people of that part of the world always show.

'Black by day, red at night', they used to say, referring to the iron furnaces and forges that covered this landscape a century ago. The name, 'Black Country', was coined about 1860 by an American, whom it struck with particular horror. To understand the landscape and its people, whose highly individual culture is born of long isolation from the rest of England, we need to know about the landscape their ancestors moved into some 1500 years ago.

From a few surviving bits we can see that before industry appeared the natural landscape was sandy and pretty sterile, and what farming there was was clearly a hard living. In fact, though there were miles of common pasture, free feeding for cattle, it was not a living at all. Fortunately, there was coal just under the surface, very near the surface – as the people soon found – and ironstone. They were leading as it were a double life, farming in spring and summer, digging coal and iron ore the rest of the year or on wet days, and so from quite early on developing the metal trades for which the Black Country has long been famous. In fact, the very word 'Smethwick', now the name of a big town, means the 'smiths' village', or the 'smiths' farm'. The smiths and the metal trades gave their name to a village perhaps 1000 years ago. Since the Black Country communities were poor, industry remained on a small scale; they made small things like nails, bolts and chains. In places it has remained on a small scale to the present day.

But there is another extremely interesting reason for the production of small things in this part of the country, and it stems from the very nature of the landscape. The Black Country is a plateau, a watershed. All the water that falls on it runs away very quickly in all directions in small streams. There are no sizeable rivers (the only means of transporting large goods in the days before canals and railways), and the nearest navigable water is the Severn at Bewdley, which is twenty to thirty miles away. The only way to get to it from the Black Country was by packhorse. Everything went out by horse, and anything people wanted came in by horse. Bewdley was the great outlet; hundreds of packhorses trailed down to the banks of the river and there were so many boats, it was said, you could hardly see the water. As this was the only way to get out, it was a very inward-looking countryside, with its own highly individual culture and its own sardonic humour.

The earliest settlement took the form of isolated hamlets on the barren heaths: places with names like Wall Heath, Blackheath, Small Heath. Looking at the huge urban expanse of West Bromwich, it is difficult to believe that Bromwich means the 'gorse farm'; this town has grown up upon a gorse-strewn heath. Hamlet joined to hamlet and grew into towns with the growth of industry. Willenhall still makes small things and is famous for its locks. It is a hub of small-scale, highly-skilled engineering, and the characteristic tall workshops of the lock-makers are hidden down narrow closes.

One of the marked exceptions to this hamlet kind of landscape was the occasional village, such as Wednesbury, now a sizeable hill-top town. The name means Woden's burh, the earthwork where Woden was worshipped in heathen times. The church is built inside the earthwork, demonstrating again the continuity of English life. I think the little place called Mushroom Green must be a sardonic local joke for a place that grew up overnight. The squatters quickly put up their cottages; all over the Black Country people 'squatted' on the commons. If they could put up a house and get the smoke coming out of the chimney in twenty-four hours it was their freehold and the lord of the manor could not turn them off. The squatter believed in this immemorial right to put up his cottage overnight, but it also suited the lord of the manor who collected a small rent, and it provided a labour force for the industrial revolution which was just getting under way. Before the growth of large industry, the workshop would be alongside the cottage: very often it was inside the home.

The landscape created by small men, by miner-farmers, a very small-scale landscape, was shaped at its other extreme by the influence of a noble family who owned about 25,000 acres on the edge of the Black Country. The Dudleys had immense mineral resources which they exploited – clay, coal, iron, limestone – everything they touched turned to money.

You could say that the Black Country was robbed, and the Dudleys were the robber barons of the eighteenth and nineteenth centuries. While helping themselves to the minerals – which, of course, they owned – they took great care to exempt themselves by legislation from making any kind of compensation for things like mining subsidence, disturbance of surface pastures, and so on. One of the most spectacular examples of subsidence due to mining is the Crooked House, a pub near Himley.

Getting the industrial goods out has always been a Black Country problem – and from the 1760s onwards a network of canals was created, revolutionising this countryside which had had no navigable water. The great problem for canal engineers in the Black Country was the very high ridge which crosses it, nearly 900 feet above sea level, of extremely hard rock, basalt mostly. It took them over twenty years before they had the courage, or perhaps the skill, to drive a tunnel through. That was the old Dudley Tunnel. The Netherton Tunnel is about the same length, just about two miles long, and was built quite late, well into the railway age, from 1855 to 1858. It was a very modern canal for the time, with a towpath on each side, and was originally lit by gas. It was a tremendous achievement. Only two tunnels were ever driven through the massive ridge. The highest, or the lowest, point was about 300 feet below the surface. In other words, the canal comes through dead level, and cuts off a tremendous rise and fall. The Netherton Tunnel is lined all the way through with very hard Staffordshire blue bricks, but even they are not waterproof.

You can also see the impact of the canal engineers on the landscape in the new kind of architecture; for instance, the engine houses for pumping and the bridges built for the horses to pass from one side of the canal to another. It was mostly coal mining at one end of the tunnel on the east side of the Black Country, and most of the ironstone and limestone came from the west. The canal, this magnificent borehole, brought the coal and iron together.

To build canals in this part of England it was necessary to climb up to a plateau nearly 500 feet above sea level. The water had to be got up to the top by a long series of locks. There were other obstacles. The plateau meant a general shortage of water so, to top up the canals as it were, there are canal reservoirs.

Primarily because of the canals a tremendous new industrial area very quickly grew up. It produced all sorts of indirect consequences: one was that this late development, with its huge increase of population, found the Anglican Church quite unprepared. There were very few Anglican churches because of the early poverty of the region – few people and no money – so the Methodists moved in to fill the need, and as a result there are, or there were, hundreds of Victorian chapels, and even the boatmen were catered for by their own little chapels. Some of the chapels are quite deserted now, some have become small workshops and factories, yet Methodism still retains a powerful hold.

Today there is only one blast furnace left working in this great iron-making district, and its days are numbered. But the Black Country itself is far from finished: even though it has lost its natural materials it has huge human reserves of skill. The old canal pattern, still very

---

35. The fact that the Black Country extends over a distinct plateau meant no navigable rivers and hence an intricate network of canals which joined up the main rivers like the Trent, the Mersey, and the Severn. Even the map (opposite), showing the canal network at its height about 1830, is somewhat simplified in the interest of clarity. The summit of the plateau was reached by a series of locks (see back cover for instance) and the main high ridges were negotiated by means of long tunnels.

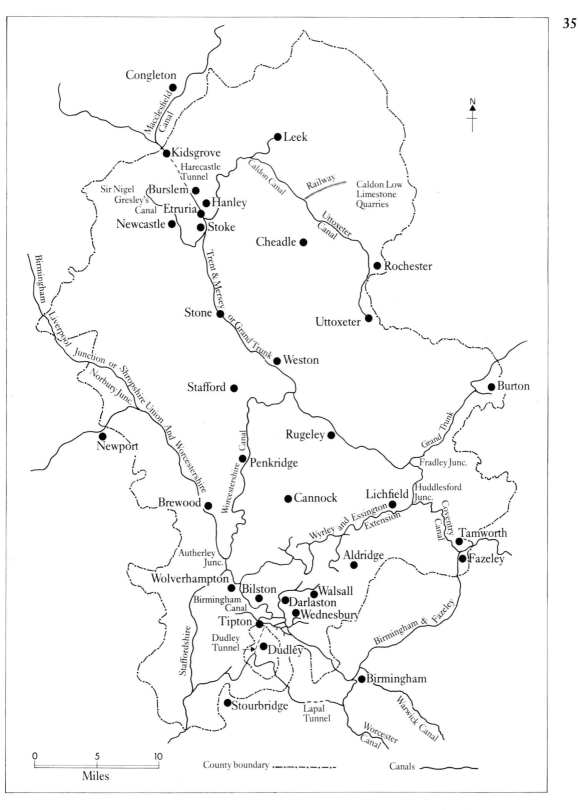

Congleton

Macclesfield Canal

Kidsgrove

Leek

Harecastle Tunnel

Caldon Canal

Railway

Caldon Low Limestone Quarries

Sir Nigel Gresley's Canal

Burslem

Hanley

Etruria

Newcastle

Stoke

Cheadle

Uttoxeter Canal

Rochester

Birmingham Liverpool Junction or Shropshire Union And Worcestershire

Norbury Junc.

Stone

Trent & Mersey or Grand Trunk

Weston

Uttoxeter

Stafford

Burton

Grand Trunk

Newport

Worcestershire Canal

Rugeley

Penkridge

Fradley Junc.

Brewood

Cannock

Lichfield

Huddlesford Junc.

Coventry Canal

Wyrley and Essington Extension

Tamworth

Autherley Junc.

Aldridge

Fazeley

Wolverhampton

Bilston

Birmingham Canal

Walsall

Darlaston

Tipton

Wednesbury

Staffordshire

Birmingham & Fazeley

Dudley Tunnel

Dudley

Birmingham

Stourbridge

Lapal Tunnel

Worcester Canal

Warwick Canal

N

0   5   10
Miles

County boundary ·—·—·—·

Canals ———

effective in places, has been superseded by an equally complicated modern road pattern. Above all, the motorways and the tremendous growth of roads and buildings of all kinds had consequences: the raw materials, especially crushed stone for the roads, have to come from somewhere. The huge quarry at Rowley Regis has produced miles of motorway, including the infamous Spaghetti Junction. I think every hole in the ground has its own story, and Rowley Regis is one of the biggest holes in the country. In some places, the waste is being pushed back into the holes from which it came, and the landscape is changing faster than ever before.

36. The Black Country was once littered with thickly-smoking blast furnaces, and was one of the chief steel-making regions of England, but the industry has died down to this one last ironworks at Bilston. The last furnace, belonging to the British Steel Corporation, was built only in the 1950s, close to the site where John Wilkinson, one of the founders of the Industrial Revolution, built his first blast furnace in 1767. It was affectionately known as Elizabeth after the daughter of a previous owner (what sort of girl was she to have a blast furnace named after her?) and was put out in November 1977. Its future is still uncertain.

37. Rowley Regis Quarry: it is a region of complicated rocks, and here the tough basalt has yielded millions of tons of road stone. There are many such vast quarries, covering, in all, one square mile, but this is by far the largest.

38. Canal and motorway near Smethwick. The land-locked Black Country was brought into contact with navigable water by an intricate system of canals in the late eighteenth century and the early nineteenth. Now it is also criss-crossed by an equally intricate pattern of motorways, including Spaghetti Junction. Here the modern motorway flies over an old cocoa-coloured canal – a study in brick and concrete.

39. The Black Country has exhausted its vast coal reserves, but underground is a world of galleries and, above, a landscape of abandoned and often flooded workings. No fewer than 15,000 disused mine-workings have been listed officially. It is, or was, a derelict landscape, characterised by sinking buildings like these, but it is only fair to say that massive efforts are being made to tidy up the ravages of the past century or so.

40. Mushroom Green is a typical squatters' settlement, so called because it sprang up almost overnight. It is a scattered collection of red-brick cottages, mostly devoted in the past to nail-making, one of the scores of minor but necessary industries of this bit of the Midlands.

6. The Deserted Midlands

The upper valley of the Thames around Lechlade has been called one of the most beautiful riverine landscapes in this country. The Thames flows out into the North Sea and it was from across the North Sea that the Old English – Anglo-Saxon, Jute and Frisian – settlers came.

They used the rivers to penetrate this unknown country; whole families with their goods and chattels were more easily transported by water, and the Thames was a major point of entry into the heart of England because it was navigable right up to the very edge of the Cotswolds. These early colonists were sensitive to the slightest rise in the ground which might indicate that they could pitch their tents above any possible flooding.

The river was in places extremely shallow, with many fords, but it rose very rapidly. Little places, like Chimney on the banks of the river, were regularly cut off each winter by floods filling the whole of the valley and the older maps show all the surrounding fields to be rough common pasture. The nearest place of any size, Bampton-in-the-Bush, is several miles back from the river. Then, as late as the 1870s, artificial cuts were made to control the river. The largest of these, the Great Brook, is a major factor in draining the land.

But a village might last 1000 years and then be overtaken by quite another kind of fate than flooding. The empty street of the village of Old Shifford, now deserted, is lined with hawthorn trees and on each side are the platforms on which the houses stood. I suppose Shifford was abandoned, or given over to grassland farming, 400 or 500 years ago. The little church, rebuilt in the Victorian style and standing close to the river, has been abandoned yet again.

At Widford, too, in the Windrush valley, the picture is typical: the church all by itself, the village gone – but beneath the church are the remains of a Roman villa. To me, this is another example of the continuity of the English landscape: there was no need to destroy an efficient Romano-British farming estate, even when the Saxons came. Although the villa itself had fallen into decay, the earliest Christian church was built upon the ruins.

The great break came later. Probably it was the same old story: the big landlord turned it all over to sheep and cattle pasture, depopulating the village. Whereas at Old Shifford evidence of the lost village can be seen in the mounds marking the street, at Widford there is a field strewn with nettles – always a sign of past human occupation. Nettles proclaim nitrogen in the soil; clusters of them must represent old habitation sites. I suppose the whole village went 400 years ago.

The agent of change was not invariably a large lay proprietor; the monasteries could be equally ruthless. Sometimes they had no choice: if a plague or pestilence depopulated a village there was insufficient labour to make a go of arable farming. Beneath the Midland pastures, the patterns of the medieval world still show through the strips of the open fields, every one of which was the basis of some individual peasant's existence.

There are hundreds of deserted villages scattered throughout England, and they are heavily concentrated in the Midlands. Why did some go and others remain? The answer in the main is that where one man, the squire, owned the manor – every house, every bit of land in it – he could change the whole economy. In another type of village – one, say, of peasant freeholders and cottagers – the law protected them. Even in the sixteenth century, when the law was as always on the side of the rich, the peasantry could appeal, and the squire could not do just as he liked. In such cases the village economy remained untouched and the village survived.

Witney is one of the most attractive little towns in Oxfordshire, and its great feature is the enormous green, dominated by the parish church. It has a weekly market, lots of shops, and one or two big annual fairs, and many of the people seen in the market-place today could be descended from the very villagers who were once evicted from their homes in the surrounding countryside. They came into towns like Witney because of the opportunities, the tremendous variety of crafts and trades which flourished there.

Not far from Witney is Wychwood Forest, still quite a big area, though only a remnant of what it used to be. Over the centuries it provided all sorts of very necessary jobs. When most implements and tools were made of wood, there was a variety of local industries in and around the Forest. Today, Wychwood is still impressive to look at and must have been even more so when it was a royal hunting forest. It is named after the Hwicce – an old English people whose territory it was some 1500 years ago.

To me, the particular distinction of this landscape is the feeling that it is in the very heart of England, absolutely lost to the world. It is mostly grassland, and what you see are not people, but cattle and sheep everywhere. It is a very lonely kind of countryside with hundreds of deserted village sites, and roads and lanes untouched for centuries.

A classic example of this loneliness is Otmoor. An extremely ancient piece of country, flat, ill-drained, with 450 feet of solid clay underneath, it takes its name from some Old English landowner. 'Otta's Moor' it was called – incidentally, the word 'moor', which we associate today with uplands, was often used in older times for any kind of bad, ill-drained, even low-lying land. Around the edge of this saucer-shaped piece of country are seven villages, and the people of every accredited farm and cottage had the right to turn their cattle out to graze on the moor for half the year. Although for the rest of the year it was under water, the common pasture right was a very valuable right indeed and the villagers owed their whole economy to it.

But in 1815 the big landlords, putting farming on a more commercial basis, began to drain the moor. They made new channels, straightened the old river, and with a new, much wider cut took the water off faster. They also created fields with straight hedgerows and, by so doing, extinguished the ancient rights which the villagers had enjoyed for more than 1000 years. Needless to say the peasants fought this bitterly – sometimes physically. They burnt the new fences, broke up the new constructions and did other damage as well. Law-suits followed and dragged on for twenty years. The judge finished up by saying in 1834 that he hoped he had heard the last of that word Otmoor.

In the middle of this empty countryside are found ancient roads which are followed by parish and even by county boundaries. The roads must have been there when parishes and counties were marked out back in the tenth century or earlier. What is interesting is that the modern road system picks up here and there bits of the ancient, winding drove-roads, then veers away in some other direction, leaving another long-lost green track.

Throughout the Midland countryside, you now see a landscape planned mostly in the eighteenth and nineteenth centuries. By Act of Parliament and special commissioners, hawthorn hedges or elm or ash trees were planted around new fields, usually of ten acres, the most efficient size for grazing. But 200 years ago there would have been only a few hedges in sight. Hedge planting brought about a revolution in the country landscape. Today, a disease brought into this country with imported timber threatens another equally radical change – 'elm disease'.

As I go around England, what impress me more than anything are the frequent changes of landscape. I am crossing the grain of the country. Different kinds of stone cross this countryside diagonally, and every few miles it shows, not only in the colour of the soil, but in the colour of the buildings. Warmington in Warwickshire is built of a lovely ironstone, which ranges from a kind of old gold to a lovely dark velvety brown. To me, Warmington is mainly the colour and the texture of its houses, but it is also what many people would think of as a typical English village, with a village pond, ducks, a great green and a manor house.

The English landscape as a whole has about a hundred landscapes inside it, like the minor themes in a great symphony. You cannot enjoy our English landscape without going back to the history behind it. Constable, the most beloved of English landscape painters, I think, sums it up: 'We see nothing till we truly understand it.'

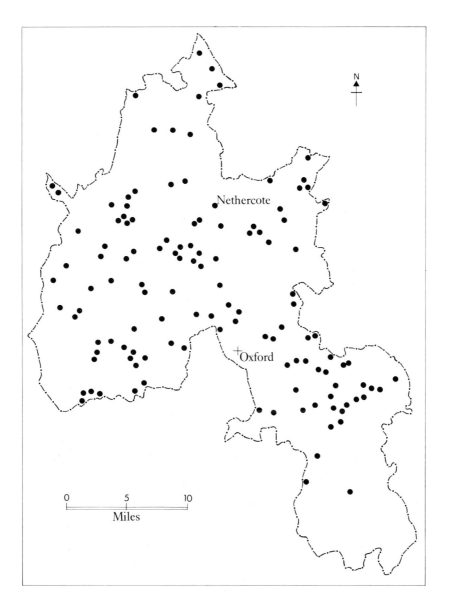

N

Nethercote

+Oxford

0   5   10
Miles

41. The Midlands as a whole show the greatest concentration of deserted villages of any part of England, and Oxfordshire, shown here, has a remarkable number of such sites. There are no fewer than 125 in this one county and fresh discoveries (such as Nethercote, marked here) will continue to be made.

42

43

64 *The Deserted Midlands*

42. Drove Road, Banbury Lane: showing a disused part of the long 'lane' which begins up in the fattening pastures of Welland valley in Leicestershire and crosses the Midlands to reach the great cattle market at Banbury in Oxfordshire. Banbury is still the largest cattle market in Europe. Here a disused part of the lane is picked up (background) by a bit of modern road.

43. The Thames in full flood in 1875: in winter the river was quite 'unregulated' until later schemes made 'cuts' which controlled these extensive floods. Here the unchecked river has actually breached the main Great Western Railway line.

44. Otmoor was, and largely is, a huge wasteland, common pasture from time immemorial. It is fringed with compact villages, but here and there, as some of the moor was drained, cottagers put up isolated houses. Otmoor has had a chequered history, including a bombing range in our own time, and now it is threatened again as a reservoir for London, that Great Wen that gobbles up rural England on all sides.

45

46

The Deserted Midlands

45. The elm was the great tree of the inner Midlands, especially towards the western side. Millions have died of the Dutch elm disease. The vales of Gloucester and Evesham are especially ravaged, but Oxfordshire (where this photograph was taken) is now seriously threatened. Most of these trees were planted by the Georgian and Victorian enclosing landlords, as hedge-timber. A whole landscape is vanishing in our own time.

46. Widford: the isolated church in the fields of the Windrush valley. The deserted village, another victim to large-scale cattle-farming in Tudor times, lies in the foreground, as can be detected by the trained eye in the hollows and the 'platforms' on which cottages formerly stood. The antiquity of farming in this part of the inner Midlands is evidenced by the fact that Widford church was built over the remains of a Romano-British villa, which presupposes a farmed estate all round here.

47. For many centuries, indeed from primeval times, the Thames, flowing in a very wide flat valley, has inundated square miles of land every winter. Not until the nineteenth century were serious attempts made to control it by means of artificial 'cuts' like this one – the Great Brook – and several other 'brooks' and 'cuts'. The Great Brook, though artificial, looks here like an old canal made centuries ago.

48. Nuneham Courtenay, Oxfordshire: this relatively small country house was a Palladian villa in the Thames valley not far from Oxford. It has a long history despite its apparent simplicity. There had been an ancient village here. The 'new highway' in 1736 was improved, but Lord Harcourt decided the old village was unsightly and had it demolished. It is sometimes thought to be the scene of Goldsmith's *The Deserted Village* ('Sweet Auburn'). A new village appeared on the London road, and instead we had the villa of 1760 and the delightful small park, drawn by Paul Sandby. In fact, the whole landscape was later changed, as described by Frank Emery in *The Oxfordshire Landscape*, and Nuneham Courtenay became a large country house and a park landscaped by Capability Brown.

7. Cornwall: Behind the Scenery

Cornwall is a county that most people think of in terms of wonderful coastal scenery: jagged headlands, cliffs, coves and a battering sea. For me, perhaps because I know it too well, this is *scenery* rather than landscape. In fact it is rather like looking at a pretty woman who has no intelligence. I expect a landscape to speak to me and to ask questions – or rather to pose problems, which merely pretty scenery does not. I look at it, like most people, and I like it, but what really interests me is what lies behind it. Can it talk to me about what I am looking at?

I do not dismiss scenery entirely. It reveals some of the geology and, of course, the way in which the landscape is shaped by man is bound to be influenced by the underlying rocks. In Cornwall what is below the surface often shows up particularly well, as with the spoil heaps of the china clay industry. They make an almost lunar landscape, which you can see twenty miles away. China clay is granite that has decomposed, so that these pits and heaps are always associated with the huge granite masses that come to the surface in Cornwall.

The Penwith peninsula which terminates in Land's End is the most westerly of these great masses of granite. Now Land's End, which I always think is a romantic name, only goes back to the fourteenth century as a recorded name, which is by my standards not a long way. After all, prehistoric men were moving up the Atlantic coast eight thousand years ago from the Western Mediterranean. I have often asked myself which piece of the Cornish coast did they see first? I doubt if it was Land's End. Land's End is the most westerly point, it is true, but close by there is another headland called, in Cornish, Tol-Pedn-Penwith which juts out to the south and is considerably higher than Land's End itself. I am pretty sure that the prehistoric traders would have seen that headland first, as a faint blue lump on their northern horizon.

Even so this coastline is still scenery – however magnificent – so what is it that makes Cornwall such a distinctive part of England? I would say that, more than any other part of England, Cornwall is a land of stone. Everything in it, everything of any age at all, is made of stone. The old buildings came out of the ground under men's feet, not from imported materials. They did not use brick in Cornwall because there was no suitable clay, and they did not use timber because in this windy climate it will not grow; so everything had to be of local stone – most economical and very often beautifully used.

To me, this is the basic difference between modern building and old building. Take, for instance, the texture of the slate-hung walls of the old houses in Padstow. *Cornish* slate of course, protecting the buildings against the wind and the rain. The occasional brick building that you do see exists because in the nineteenth century railways and canals brought in building materials, bricks chiefly, from distant parts, and a good deal of Welsh slate also from just across the water. But if you go back to the beginning you have to think of people becoming aware of the stone that lay under their own feet and granite is the most obvious feature of the Cornish landscape. Its use goes back perhaps four or five thousand years. To begin with it was just picked up off the open moorland – its original name was *moorstone* – you picked it up off the surface of the moor and you built your walls with it: boundary walls that go back to the Iron Age and some, I think, even to the Bronze Age. At Cape Cornwall, there are little Bronze Age fields bounded by granite walls that have not been shifted in all that time. They are very difficult to date, obviously; they are dry-stone walls, but excavation has produced evidence of their age.

By the farm of Porthmeor are mounds of masonry, now overgrown, that are the remains of an Iron Age village. It has been professionally excavated and shown to have been abandoned in the fifth or sixth century. The present farm of Porthmeor is actually a resettlement, probably in the Middle Ages, but the field pattern did not change. It retained its identity, simply because of the massiveness of the boundary walls. They remained untouched as shelter for the cattle against the almost ceaseless wind. You can also see the moorstone used in the cornerstones of farm buildings, steps, stiles, and, not least, great solitary stones in the middle of a field, still very practically used as rubbing posts for cattle but possibly prehistoric in origin.

The number of granite buildings in Cornwall, indeed all the other things made of granite, probably outnumbers those to be found in the whole of the rest of Britain. For centuries, we even had to cross granite bridges over the River Tamar to get into this land of stone. The Tamar is the frontier between England and Cornwall. When the Cornish came up this way they often made their wills before they started, for England was a foreign country. Grey-stone Bridge over the Tamar, built in 1439, still carries heavy modern traffic. Among other things, apart from telling us that granite is the great building stone of Cornwall, it should also dispel the myth that medieval roads were poor and nearly impassable. Why should you build a bridge like that if the roads on both sides were as bad as the books say? They were not, of course.

These bridges are the grand gateways into Cornwall, but the Tamar is almost a national boundary. The Cornish are very distinctive as a people, and they have a culture of their own. For example, you notice a tremendous number of original place-names which have never been changed, which show that the Cornish remain, basically, an unconquered people.

Most of the Cornish villages, like Altarnun for example, have Celtic names. Altarnun means in fact 'the altar of St Nonna' – a Celtic saint coming from Wales and supposed to have been the mother of St David. The primitive cross in a Cornish churchyard indicates the earliest evidence of the preaching place, in so many Cornish parishes, of a Celtic missionary priest from Ireland or Wales – the great centres of culture in the so-called Dark Ages. The cross at Altarnun marks the spot where St Nonna stood and preached the gospel: the church came long afterwards when the community had grown big enough to need one, but the site was already a hallowed one. Gradually hundreds of communities built their own churches. I always regard the parish church as England's special contribution to the man-made landscape, not only in Cornwall but everywhere.

It is easy to talk about the use of granite in buildings and especially in churches, but it is in fact one of the most difficult of rocks to cut and shape. The Celtic cross at Michaelstow is a thousand years old but it shows the beginnings of the shaping of granite. A simple circle and so on. The parish church near by is still very plain and poor. It was a poor parish probably, but the church does show at least the great advance from the rough masonry of field walls to squared stone.

Gradually stone-masons' tools must have improved, and you get the possibility of granite being intricately carved and shaped. In the 1520s, for example, a superb granite church tower at Probus was built. In my view it is equal to anything you can find in, say, Somerset, that county of wonderful towers, but there they had much easier building stones to deal with. Probus church tower is just granite, and it is magnificently cut. Somehow between Michaelstow in the 1300s and Probus in the 1500s, men discovered how to do things with granite to produce really decorative effects. Granite gradually became a stone that could be shaped artistically and no longer a straightforward utilitarian material. Another masterpiece in carved granite is the south porch of St Mary Magdalene at Launceston.

The Cornish tin-miners also used granite very widely, for their engine-houses and other buildings. As a result these have become lasting monuments to a now almost dead industry, an industry which nevertheless changed the landscape all round it. From Botallack Mine, which overhangs the Atlantic Ocean in the extreme west of the Penwith peninsula, some of the shafts actually went out a long way under the sea. On stormy days miners working down below could hear the boulders being rolled about on the sea bed above. I have heard it myself in a nearby mine and it is not a pleasant sound.

Cornwall is not all granite by any means. At Catacleuse Point near Padstow is a cliff quarry, a common feature of the Cornish coast. Just looking around it you can see how the colour of the local slate depends upon how much weathering it has had. In some lights it comes out as a lovely pale blue, sometimes it is a nice shade of grey, and it can also appear at times to be black. Different colours, depending upon how much exposure to the sea and the weather, and at Catacleuse it is a very exposed headland indeed. The quarry is disused now, but I keep a few nice pieces of Catacleuse stone in my study as paperweights.

St Merryn church is about three miles inland from the Catacleuse quarries with its lovely arcade of bluey-grey stone which must have been specially chosen for its quality. The pillars of the arcade are smooth, but what we call the fillets, the bands between the mouldings, are, when you touch them, as sharp as the day they were cut five hundred years ago. In the same church there is a superb thirteenth-century font, Catacleuse stone again, but nearly black in a bad light. But the really lovely thing is the interior as a whole. Above all, the arcades, so unexpected in the beauty of their colouring after the austere outside.

Some of the most beautiful things in Cornwall have come from quarries that are now so overgrown that you might not know they are there; all that remains is a deep pool and a mossy track up which the blocks of stone were once dragged by teams of men and horses.

The quarry near Polyphant is one of the smallest in Cornwall. It is quite deserted – a beautiful setting; I suppose they stopped quarrying about a hundred years ago. There are pits all round. The stone is called Polyphant, after the name of the hamlet. It is very unpromising to look at on the ground; but when it has been polished by craftsmen, it comes up a beautiful dove grey. It is used in church towers, arcades and above all, in the neighbourhood, in headstones – some beautiful Polyphant headstones you can find round here, such as the superb one – almost a kind of marble – which reads:

'Death with his Dart, Did pierce my Heart When I was in my Prime
Vain World adieu, My Parents too 'Twas God's Appointed time'.

Well, I love old quarries, and perhaps my appointed time will arrive somewhere at the bottom of a deserted quarry.

Slate makes up a great deal of the Cornish scene, though not as much as granite. But much of the county's buildings do consist of slate, especially the roofing, very characteristic Cornish roofing. On page 78 you can see it used in an old farmhouse at Trebarwith, close to Tintagel. A mile or two away a whole community grew up, now called Delabole, entirely dependent on the remarkable slate they found there. The quarry has been used for many hundred years, certainly since the 1550s. If you go there you see what is often said to be the biggest hole in the ground in Britain. It is about five hundred feet deep, about a mile around and it is still being used. It used to be, if you read the old guide books, 'an animated scene'. A thousand men used to work in and round the quarry bringing up a hundred and twenty tons of slate a day and cutting it for different purposes. They were not creating scenery – in fact they were destroying it – but they were also making a new landscape. Delabole slate went for roofing thousands of houses and for building hundreds of miles of field walls.

Of course Delabole was just the best-known place where they got out the slate in big quantities, but the slate extends for miles, and to enormous depths. It comes right out on the coast near there, and forms the cliff face. It is a hell of a coast. It is as hard as granite, as hard as iron, and yet there was actually a small port, Port William, I think named after William IV when the Delabole quarries were bringing their slate down to be shipped off in the 1830s. It was a little port in this iron-bound coast and it really is a hellish coast at high tide. God help any ship that got caught on it. You cannot imagine there was ever a port in such a place. At low tide it is quite different. I think ships were beached there and loaded from the track down to the cove which must have been specially made to get the slate down. It is a battered coast and whatever was there once has been smashed by the sea and now nothing is left but a wild coastal scene. But if you look carefully you can still see traces of the old iron rails embedded in the rock.

Right on the Lizard peninsula – the most southerly part of Britain – we find a stone that you have probably never heard of outside Cornwall. It is called Serpentine, and at Kynance Cove there are whole cliffs of this. Serpentine probably gets its name from the supposed resemblance of its streaks and colours to those of a serpent's skin. In fact it contains a large share of silicate of magnesium. Dull words, but for this reason the Lizard soils are very poor. Little will grow on them except *Erica Vagans* – a heathland plant which is unique in its tolerance of magnesium in the stony soil. In fact, unique in England: here then the natural vegetation precisely maps the underlying rock.

Serpentine stone was not used much for buildings – it was probably too hard – but you will find some in the local churches. At Landewednack church near the Lizard it is used in the tower, but mixed with a lighter coloured granite which produces a kind of chequerboard effect. Serpentine forms the backbone of the Lizard – it juts out so far into the Channel that Marconi used it to receive his first transatlantic radio messages from Newfoundland. It is a historic place, and a monument now commemorates it.

What makes the Serpentine rock even more interesting is that it has certain qualities which make it particularly useful for modern scientific purposes. Up on the top, on the back of the Lizard, it is dead flat and to some people a dreary scene, but not to me. You see coming towards you great saucers on the top of the land. They are picking up messages from satellites more than 22,000 miles out in space. Their position is superb – nothing is in the way – but the site was not chosen just for that. These giant saucers carry a tremendous weight so they are built upon a thousand solid feet of Serpentine rock, because it will not give; and above all, the Serpentine was found to provide the least interference with the minute signals that these saucers pick up. As a comparison, it is rather like detecting on Earth the heat of a one-bar electric fire lit on the moon. A road sign suddenly brings it home to you that the Earth is not just a word – it puts us in our place. Beside a lonely Cornish by-road a sign says simply *Earth Station: Goonhilly*.

There are people who think Goonhilly is a blot on the natural landscape. Well, I don't. I think – though I hate modern technology in general – that Goonhilly is one of the most marvellous sites in England. What caps it all is the way that as you approach these immense saucers there are the circular barrows – the burial mounds of Bronze Age men. It is the combination of these burial mounds four thousand years old and Goonhilly Earth Station which is to me a magnificent conjunction of the ancient world and the future. Goonhilly is obviously not just scenery: it is pure landscape and as deeply moving as any landscape fashioned a thousand or so years ago. Goonhilly at sunset, with no man in sight, silently listening all the time to the most remote signals. It is a scene that would have inspired Thomas Hardy.

49. Padstow: quayside houses built of granite or slate and hung with overlapping slates on all the weather sides. Such a protection can be found in many places in south-western England. Cornwall especially is the land of wind and rain.

50. Greystone Bridge over the Tamar: a superb granite bridge linking Devon and Cornwall, or rather, the Cornish would say, linking England to Cornwall. It is rather older than used to be thought, as Bishop Lacy (of Exeter, in whose diocese it lay) granted an indulgence on 27 December 1439 for the construction and repair of the bridge under this name. It carried the main road from Launceston to Tavistock, both important towns, and still does.

51. Botallack Mine: perched right over the Atlantic Ocean, this mine began producing tin and copper as far back as 1721 and was once a scene of great and dangerous industry. It gradually ceased work in the middle decades of the nineteenth century with the discovery of richer lodes in Malaysia (tin) and copper in South Africa and South America. Cornish miners emigrated in their thousands, all over the mineral world, so much so that there is a saying that wherever there is a hole in the ground you will find a Cornishman at the bottom of it. The Botallack Mine extended far out under the sea and was 1200 feet deep. The remains are accessible but need great care in approaching them.

52. Trebarwith, near Tintagel: a Cornish farmhouse built of the local slate from top to bottom. Probably Elizabethan in date. Usually the slate roof was given a thick coating of cement to make it all completely weather-proof.

53. Delabole: this enormous hole is the product of over 400 years of slate-quarrying.

54. Goonhilly Earth Station: these huge saucers are tracking particular satellites more than 22,000 miles out in space. In most landscapes they would dominate and ruin the scene, but not here, where the vast heaths of the Lizard peninsula reduce them to scale.

55. Probus: the superb granite tower in the Somerset style. The church was built in the early sixteenth century and dedicated to St Probus and St Grace.

56. Altarnun: on the edge of Bodmin Moor. Cornwall was slowly converted to Christianity by missionaries from Ireland and Wales from the fifth century onwards, before Augustine ever reached the shores of Kent. At first the missionary preached by the side of a crude cross like this, and people gathered in the open air. Here St Nonna, reputedly the mother of St David, preached and possibly erected a primitive altar. The name Altarnun means 'the altar of Non or Nonna'. Later, as the community grew, a church was erected as we see here, but the primitive cross still stands in the churchyard as a reminder of the first Christian saint to preach the gospel on this spot.

8. Leicestershire:
The Fox and the Covert

The English countryside was not specially created for the fox-hunting fraternity, though they may think so; it was created at various times for quite different purposes, but what is particularly fascinating is how over the years the hunting people adapted it and used it in all sorts of ways for their own ends.

To begin with, hunting took place in an almost untouched natural landscape. Surrounded by an early medieval wall, a piece of the original hunting England survives at Bradgate in Leicestershire. Nearly 500 feet above sea level, it is a thin soil cover, over old hard rocks; natural oak woodland and bracken which is not much good for farming except in patches. It was set aside as a deer park in the twelfth century when hunting was confined first of all to deer, which was a royal animal, and secondly confined to a very limited class of people. That is the reason for the wall which is about four and a half miles around – it kept the deer in and the peasantry out. The king initially kept this right to hunt deer to himself; later on he granted licences to magnates – the great men of the region – to have their own deer parks, but what is rather special about Bradgate Park is how it has come down to this day almost untouched.

As time went on the great men who owned these old deer parks usually built themselves a grand house. Bradgate House was built by Thomas Grey, Marquis of Dorset, and was one of the earliest country houses to be finished in England. It was finished by about 1502, and the Greys lived there for generations. One of the names we know is that of the unfortunate Lady Jane Grey, who was born here and was beheaded in 1554, as every schoolchild knows, Queen of England for nine days only, the innocent victim of high politics. They say that the oaks in this park were pollarded when the news was brought to Bradgate that she had been beheaded in London. I think this most unlikely – a later myth.

The Tudor gentry, especially the early Tudors, preferred the pleasures of hunting to the trouble and bother of farming. They were still living in the medieval past. The English nobility and gentry were mad about hunting, and throughout the country hundreds of parks existed solely for the pleasure of the privileged few. The Greys continued at Bradgate House until about 1720, then moved to another big house in Staffordshire. They abandoned Bradgate completely, and the park remains to this day in its original natural state.

In High Leicestershire, as it is called, in the north-east of the county, we can place the next step in the evolution of hunting. For centuries the only animal to be hunted seriously was the deer. You hear nothing about hunting the fox or the hare; the hare was good for the peasantry to eat, the fox was simply chased because it was regarded as vermin and it gave a good run and so on. The first record of fox-hunting occurs in a curious place: in an account book at Belvoir Castle there is an entry in the autumn of 1539 which simply records 'the payment of money for meat and drink to certain poor people for finding the fox when my lord was hunting at Sproxton'. And it must have been over heathland because this piece of country, though it is now mostly cultivated, is still marked on the map as this so-and-so heath and that. The first reference to hares is about the same date, at a place a few miles further away, Bescaby Closes, where again a payment is made to poor village people for finding hares when the Earl of Rutland and his retinue went out coursing.

Bescaby today is a very attractive spot – grassland mainly, with signs of the lost village just visible as humps in the field. They chased the hare there because it was a deserted landscape. The fields had been enclosed, turned over to grass, and it belonged to the Earl of Rutland who could do what he liked with it. The now-beautiful moated site, overgrown with trees, probably had a house on it at one time, but today Bescaby is completely lost. It is a job to find it even on the one-inch map, but it marked the beginnings of records relating to hunting foxes and hares.

So fox-hunting developed in Leicestershire more than 400 years ago and it continues to this day. East Leicestershire has been substantially grassland for most of that time. There is less of it now only because in two World Wars – especially the last one – large areas were ploughed up. Still the typical scene is one of undulating grassland giving you fast runs and long unimpeded gallops. Naturally enough fox hunters have never liked cultivated land – they still don't. There was one Master of fox hounds who was asked about hunting over arable land. 'What,' he said, 'hunt over ploughed land? I'd sooner read a book.' So the great thing about this countryside was the large tract of country sown with grass because that was what the soil was best suited for. The heavy liassic clays cover most of the East Midlands, which is why these parts abound in grassland. But they have not always been as you see them today. In the late eighteenth century and the early nineteenth came the age of the parliamentary enclosures which produced the planned pattern of fields that we now see. It was then found by farming experience that a ten-acre field was the most economic size for grazing cattle. Now this planned landscape might have put a stop to the long unimpeded gallops of the old open fields, but these changes did not all come about at once, and for this reason: when certain parishes like those in the Vale of Belvoir were enclosed in the 1790s and round about then, the land was mostly owned by really big landlords who loved their hunting. The biggest of them all was the Duke of Rutland (the earls had become dukes by then). At the enclosures his share in different parishes was several hundred acres in each, and he and other great landlords like him made sure of leaving large areas without internal hedges, so that they could still have huge gallops over open country and grassland. This was unquestionably within the power of a wealthy landlord like the Duke of Rutland, who was like a king in his own country. James I, back in 1603, stayed at Belvoir Castle on his way south to London. Looking at the view from the terrace, everything he could see belonged to the Duke. 'By God,' James remarked, 'what a traitor the man would make . . .'

Later on, especially when the Dukes began to create new farms and to let the farms to tenant farmers, both landlords and farmers wanted a more efficient management of grazing, and the ten-acre field then became the recognised size. That meant the construction of miles of new hedges. The hunting people must have thought that the creation of thousands of miles of hedges following enclosure would be the end of their sport. They got over that difficulty. But what came next was a sort of multiplication of hedges close together – narrow fields and then the hedges come quite quickly – you sort of jump one and immediately find yourself heading for the next one. They had a name for this – they called it 'Pewy' country, because it reminded them (not that they ever went to church probably) of those box pews in Georgian churches. And it required a different kind of skill, much more jumping and less fast galloping down long slopes. But the horses and the men adapted themselves to this new kind of hunting. Some of the real heavyweight chaps went through a hedge and not over it, and you were probably a mighty hunter if you could get through on the other side without killing yourself or the horse. But though it looks very difficult country to hunt over, they succeeded in maintaining the sport.

The hedges themselves differed quite a lot. They were all artificially planted, except the old parish boundaries. The new ones consisted, in this part of England, of posts and rails with seedling thorn trees planted against them. And some landlords put up a double post and rail with the seedling trees planted in between. It takes about twenty years for that kind of hedge to grow strong enough to keep the cattle in, which is after all its real use. In that time some hedges became enormous and formidable obstacles.

One of the distinctive little features in this landscape was the creation of special covers or coverts by big landlords for the purpose of giving the foxes a chance to breed, and also, of course, for the Hunt to know where to find them when they wanted to. This bit of England is covered with these patches of woodland with characteristic and sometimes odd names.

Thorpe Trussels, in the country of the Quorn Hunt, is one of the most famous of the fox covers in Leicestershire. Thorpe is the name of the nearest village, and Trussels is a dialect word meaning a small piece of land – an odd pocket. It has a very interesting origin. When the parish of Thorpe Satchville was enclosed in the late eighteenth century the commissioners had to allot ten acres of land as a cow pasture to the poor, who, as usual, got the dirty end of the stick. The land they got was on the edge of the parish and very poor

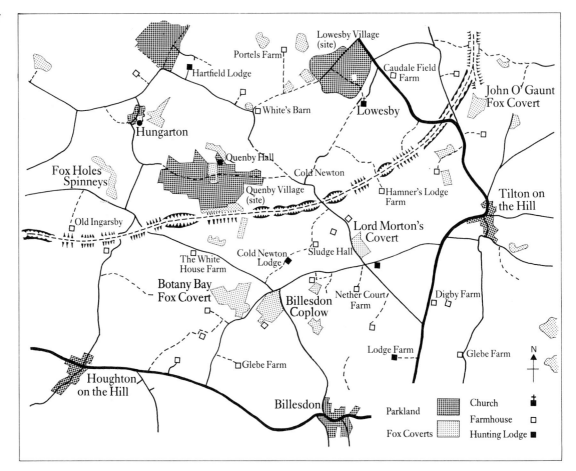

57 and **58.** Fox coverts and hunting lodges in the heart of the Quorn country. Many farm-houses were virtually 'lodges' also in the season.

indeed, but they found the right solution to this; they rented it to the Quorn Hunt for thirty-five pounds a year. The Quorn were glad to get it and planted it up as a thick fox cover. The poor were happy because the thirty-five pounds a year went on providing coal for the parish. So both rich and poor were satisfied with this rough justice.

Botany Bay covert gives itself away by its name, the date 1790–ish. Again it was on the frontiers of a parish and so far away from human habitation that it got this kind of joke name after the convict settlement in Australia. One of the most striking Leicestershire landmarks right beside it is Billesdon Coplow. It rises to six hundred feet, with a characteristic shape, and many a lost huntsman has found his way home in the dusk from here by using it as a landmark. You had to have these special artificial covers created by big landlords or by big hunts because Leicestershire, and to some extent Rutland, had long been

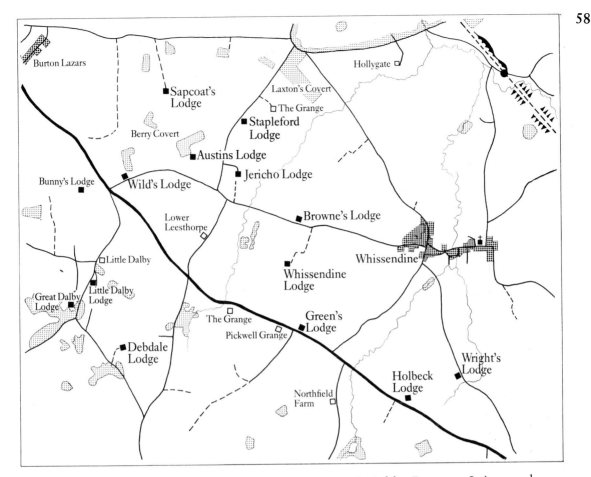

denuded of natural woodland. Another historic cover is Ashby Pastures. It is very dense, and apart from a pathway or two almost continuous cover. All these had to be specially planted.

Early fox-hunting was really rather casual in the sense that people formed parties and went out from some big house or other. There must have been rough and ready rules but they only got properly organised in the early eighteenth century. The real history of fox-hunting, of organised fox-hunting with strict rules, is nearly always attributed to (and I think rightly) Hugo Meynell who was the first Master of what became the famous Quorn Hunt: the most expensive and exclusive Hunt in this country. As you might expect, the Quorn had sharp social distinctions. The country over which they hunted was really of two different kinds. The classic country was long rolling grassland, but to the westward across the rather insignificant River Soar the territory degenerated or, if you like, changed into something much wilder and rougher. The Monday and the Friday Hunt were the exclusive ones for the best hunting – faster and so on – and another day, Tuesday, was left to what the rich, the real Quorn people, called 'the local people'. So you had in the Quorn country nice social distinctions and also two different hunting landscapes, and you belonged to one or the other.

Pretty well every change in the landscape roused the wrath of the fox-hunting people. Railways, they thought, would really put paid to their sport by establishing dangerous and impassable barriers. In fact, the railways probably enhanced the sport because men could then travel from wider distances and bring in their hunters with them.

The map of this bit of country shows a great number of the smaller special-purpose buildings, called so-and-so Lodge. These were put up by all sorts of people for the hunting season. You find them dotted all over this piece of countryside – scores of them within a mile or two. Some were quite modest, others were large because rich families moved in with a number of servants and occupied them for the hunting season. The best of these is probably Warwick Lodge, in Melton Mowbray itself. It was named after the Countess of Warwick, one of Edward VII's mistresses, who hunted fiercely. It is now the District Council Offices – a characteristic change, as is the petrol pump in the stable yard where she kept her hunters.

The hunting world also created special-purpose buildings which had never before been seen in the countryside. They were for the big rich hunts like the Quorn and the Cottesmore, and comprised stables for the horses and kennels for the hounds. There are a couple of lovely examples of this in Leicestershire and Rutland. The Cottesmore hunt put up very large stables and kennels in 1890 just outside the little town of Oakham – huge brick buildings, looking to me rather like a cross between a prison and a workhouse, but typical late Victorian architecture. Then the Quorn, which was rolling in money, put up even larger kennels and stables miles away from the Cottesmore country, at a place called Pawdy Lane. That was in 1905. The total cost was £14,000 which you would have to multiply twenty times over I think, to get the equivalent sum of money today. They were a rich lot and they could easily afford out of their spare cash to create these special-purpose buildings – the peak, to me anyway, of vulgar, ostentatious Edwardian England.

Well, the hunting still goes on – in fact it flourishes – but the famous grasslands of East Leicestershire have diminished in size. A lot have come back since the end of the war, reconverted to grass, but the total area is rather less. I do not think it matters terribly – there is still plenty of room in what is basically a rather lonely countryside, in which church steeples can be seen from miles away. Not for nothing did steeplechasing start here.

So this landscape was created for all sorts of reasons, some almost accidental. You start off with a natural landscape – the deer park at Bradgate; fox-hunting and hare-coursing developed over the natural heathland; and then the landscape changed for farming reasons in the late eighteenth century, and hunting people, in a way, took it over and adapted it. So the landscape here is dotted with historic names that stir the heart of hunting people all over the Midlands: the Whissendine Brook, Billesdon Coplow, Ashby Pastures, Melton Mowbray – that Mecca of hunting, as it was, anyway. There is a galaxy of sacred names.

59. Bescaby in deepest Leicestershire: the village was abandoned for more profitable cattle and sheep farming probably about 1500. The site of the old village can still be seen in faint hump and hollows but the remains of the small moated house (or rather its moat, as seen here) are clear enough. Because it offered tracts of pasture uninterrupted by any difficult arable, we get the beginnings of fox-hunting and of hare-coursing here in the early 1500s.

60

61

88　Leicestershire: The Fox and the Covert

Broadgate in Leicestershire Being the Seate of ỹ Rᵗ Honᵇˡᵉ the Earle of Stamford.

60. The richer hunts – like the Quorn, the Cottesmore, and the Pytchley (in Northants) – built their own stables and kennels in the late nineteenth century and the early twentieth. These, the Quorn kennels, were special purpose-built buildings in red brick, with a characteristic cupola and clock, redolent of the vulgar days which ended in 1914.

61. Fields and hedges of typical hunting country in East Leicestershire ('the Quorn Country') – a landscape planned in the closing years of the eighteenth century.

62. Bradgate House and Park: Bradgate is still one of the most original medieval hunting parks in England, since it was never 'landscaped'. This drawing by Knyff, done about 1710, shows the great Tudor house while it was still lived in, the formal gardens, and the untouched park beyond.

9. Derbyshire: No Stone Unturned

When you look at the peaks and the valleys of Derbyshire today, if you know where to look, you can see the landscape of two industries, both of them in a rural setting, and at first sight an apparently formless scene. There is the limestone plateau high up, and over it the cold upland wind flows unchecked: this is the dead landscape of lead mining. Down in the lusher valley is the landscape of another industry brought to these parts about two hundred years ago, and based on water power. Each industry was a revolution producing its own peculiar landscape; and in a curious hidden way they are linked together.

If you came across one of the mining scenes by accident in a lonely bit of countryside, without knowing what it was, you would be willing to bet it was some natural catastrophe, some geological convulsion. In fact, the whole thing has been made by man and is the work of the old lead miners. They found the traces of lead on the surface – it shows itself in the vegetation, so they knew exactly where to start digging – and they dug down. They left kinds of rugged openings called rakes; upland Derbyshire is criss-crossed with hundreds of them. One of the most spectacular is Dirtlow Rake, near Castleton. I think it probably started at the top in Roman times, because not far away a Roman ingot of lead has been found, and at intervals it has been re-opened and dug deeper and deeper.

At what they call the cheek of the vein, for a considerable distance, you have actually got exposed the pick marks made by small-scale miners, each of whom had staked his claim to a piece of ground, exactly as in the nineteenth century with gold claims. You can see these original pick marks very clearly considering that they have been exposed to the weather for centuries. Down below, I am told, underground, you can actually see them as freshly made as though they were made yesterday. On the surface, of course, they are considerably smoothed out by wind and rain.

What is so extraordinary is that men working with picks on this apparently tiny scale could produce such a dramatic result, looking like a massive convulsion of nature. The Derbyshire rakes can be followed for mile after mile across the plateau, forming a very complicated pattern on the map. In effect you are really following long-running faults in the limestone that were once filled in with very narrow veins of lead ore. These were deposited long ago when mineral solutions welled up through the fault from deep inside the earth. Lead has been dug from these pits for some two thousand years, as an almost precious metal.

When the Saxons, for example, established the village of Youlgreave, they were aware of already existing mines because Youlgreave means 'old working'. So if it was old to them, they were almost certainly mining the veins which the Romans had started long before them. When you see how much of Derbyshire has been dug and mined for lead, you wonder where it all went. But it was, of course, the perfect roofing material for monasteries, country houses and churches all through the centuries.

At Magpie mine near Sheldon, we see what most of us would regard as a typical modern mine, although it is in ruins. The headgear shows that mining was finally abandoned only recently though. Before that the mine had been worked for over 300 years.

Generally mining went on for centuries in a small way, and this has produced a marvellous industrial landscape in a completely country setting. Near the village of Bonsall you can see this beautifully. This little bit of country is littered with stone and every piece of stone means something: it is a landscape created by small miners. They established their claims to mine in a very interesting way: by law, they had to take a sample dish of ore to the Barmaster and if he was satisfied, the miner could stake his claim to thirty yards of ground. You can still see the actual lead ore, and all around the remains of the buildings and the shafts, sixty or eighty feet deep, down which the miner worked – mostly now covered by beehive piles of stones. Every few yards you find the walls of what used to be little huts known as 'coes', where the miner would come up from his village, change his clothes and pick up his working tools. There is a kind of thirty-yard pattern of pits and heaps of stone produced by this medieval law. It does not show up clearly on the ground – it all looks a muddle; but it begins to make real sense from the air. Then you see there *is* a pattern, and a very extensive one. To use an awful cliché, the old miners literally left no stone unturned.

But you could not mine a mineral such as lead without creating the problem of pollution. We know all about lead poisoning today but so did the old Derbyshire miners. Since the landscape of the high plateau had long been denuded of trees for building and fuel for smelting, almost all the trees you see now have been planted as an anti-pollution measure. They follow the lines of the old lead workings right across the landscape. Incidentally, these straight lines of trees are very dangerous to hikers, because the old shafts, as in Cornwall, are often hidden by dead vegetation and rotten branches. The workings cut right across rich grassland, and the grass near the workings was lethal, so trees were planted to prevent the poisoning of the grazing animals. They did not directly keep the animals away from the workings, but they created a shade which kept the grass down. In that way the animals consumed less grass, less contamination, and hence avoided poisoning themselves.

Centuries ago mining and farming could not be considered entirely separately. We are so used today to the idea that everybody is a specialist in one thing only that we easily forget this. In fact, the miner was very likely to be a farmer as well on the side, and near the village of Winster we find a splendid example of this coming-together of the two major occupations of mankind, the miner-cum-farmer.

I used to think that this dual economy was based on the fact that you worked on the farm in spring and summer, and below ground in winter. It was not as simple as that. The general rule, if you could follow it, was six hours below ground and six hours above ground all the year round. But of course you had to adapt yourself to the seasons. In summer, at harvest time, you spent more time above ground. And in winter it was sometimes impossible to carry on mining because the underground water level rose, and mining stopped. That was the kind of economy they lived in, and all around here is the visible evidence of what they left behind. You find a sequence of barns and each barn represents an old miner-farmer household, and you also have, on the whole, a landscape of very small fields. They used to keep a few cows, a sheep or two, and grow some oats, both for themselves and the horses, which were the main power of the region. While they remain, and being small they are very vulnerable to modern change, the fields and the little barns take us right back to a way of life that has long ago disappeared – an age-old dual economy.

There is another bit of landscape history on Curbar Edge, where it is possible to see a number of sunken packhorse tracks. Trains of packhorses, forty or fifty strong, each carrying up to two hundredweight of lead, would have crossed these moors. Primitive bridges were put up to cross streams and at intervals, when there was not a stream or a bridge to aim at, you would find small standing stones that gave you the next siting point, aiming at the great lead market at Chesterfield.

Often the only trace of an old smelting site today is a large pond on these great empty moors. At Stone Edge the smelter chimney still stands; they say it is the oldest industrial chimney in the world. It is a miracle it is still here when you think about all the destruction and pulling down we do these days for precious little reason. Smelting produced even greater pollution than mining, so the soil all around here is still poisoned. As evidence of this you can see a plant called leadwort, because it tolerates a level of lead that few other plants can. It grows profusely on the poisoned soil where it has no competition.

Acres of land around the old smelters were made derelict. These remote high locations, often called Bole hill after the local name Bole for a smelter, were chosen, not to avoid populated areas, but simply to catch all the available wind for the primitive furnaces.

From the gritstone edge you can look across to the limestone hills which were always plagued by the problem of underground water. Now this is very strange when you consider that limestone is permeable. In fact, the plateau itself looks and is bone dry since all rainwater goes straight through it, until it reaches underground beds of lava, which hold the water. For centuries this water-table restricted really deep mining. But from the 1600s on, a simple though expensive remedy was found. We know quite a lot about this now, through the explorations of local mining historians with their special gear. Long narrow tunnels called soughs were dug into the hills from the valley floor to drain off the trapped water. Some of these soughs are miles long. They cost twenty to thirty thousand pounds even two hundred years ago, but they could pay for themselves many times over in a matter of years if they released water from a rich untapped vein. So the age of the small miner slowly passed, and that of the rich capitalists began.

From each of the soughs, and there are hundreds of them, millions of gallons of water still pour each day into the Derbyshire rivers. Two hundred years ago this water which was such an embarrassment to the lead industry was tamed, and became the basis of another great Industrial Revolution. The soughs kept the rivers replenished even in a dry season.

With its unfailing supply of water the Derwent and its tributaries were regarded by some eighteenth-century entrepreneurs as the ideal place for their new mills. The underlying basis was, of course, water power. It is easy to talk about *water power*, the words just trip off the tongue like an old cliché, but here you can see what the power really means.

At Calver Mill, the River Derwent has been diverted into a leat and the whole river scenery manipulated. It finishes up, so far as this mill is concerned, with a tremendous fall of water: this is the visible power of water, now running to waste. It is such a magnificent source of power that properties were actually advertised – rather like an estate agent's selling point – with 'water power available'.

Almost the entire length of the Derwent and its tributaries, like the Wye, was transformed by this demand for power. Though you would never believe it today, looking at the beautiful stillness of the old millponds, contemporaries regretted what they thought was the end of the old fast-flowing, shallow rippling rivers they had known. The Honourable John Byng toured these parts in 1790 and he said, 'These vales have lost all their beauties. The stream perverted from its course by sluices and aqueducts will no longer ripple and cascade. Every rural sound is sunk in the clamours of cotton works.' At one time the same water drove each mill in turn, as it passed down the valley: a simple case of multiple use. Now the valley is a series of ruins, blocked weirs, leats, and disused ponds.

Cressbrook Cotton Mill was started about 1785 before the days when mill-owners realised that the mill needed only to have a functional appearance. At first sight it looks like an eighteenth-century country house, with its classical pediment and its little bell tower. The bell tower is interesting because it goes back to the days before workers had watches and clocks. Wordsworth says something like this: 'And at the appointed hour, a bell is heard, the local summons to unceasing toil.' Later on it became a factory hooter moaning over a sleeping town, not a gentle bell across the fields.

Where for centuries there had been just village corn-mills, there were now what the Americans would call 'company towns'. The new mills also needed an army of workers for the machinery. Such a work force had to be found, and then housed. The workers' houses at Cromford are very well built. Men like Arkwright, building their great mills, needed hundreds of workers in a rather thinly populated countryside, so they had to build houses to attract a labour force, almost a new town. Arkwright also created a market-place for the new population. The great industrialists were not the ruthless builders of slums that the books used to suggest. Arkwright, and other men of his time, like Strutt, built very good housing for their workers: stone-built and solid. The slums are a different thing altogether: they came forty years later when land was getting scarce and the speculative builder moved in, with no regard to quality. To this day you can still see something of the company town, the one that Arkwright created out of the tiny village of Cromford, or another at Milford.

And he not only built houses, but also made a canal to handle his bulky products. Everything was taken care of, and like that other great man, Strutt, down at Milford, Arkwright even provided a church for his workers. At the heart of the new community, of course, was the mill, built more like a fortress than a factory. Or, as John Byng perceptively said, like 'a man of war'; that is to say the battleship of his time. After all, this factory was taking work from hundreds of independent families, who might well turn out rough and attack it: and independent men and women did not take kindly to unresting machinery and factory discipline. Arkwright's mill was designed with windows high up above the pavement to withstand an attack from angry working people. And it was not the only battle the mill owners could not afford to lose. With a huge investment in machinery and a non-stop supply of water they could not afford to let their mills stop, at least not for such a simple matter as sticking to the hours of daylight. This is another of the curious unexpected revolutions in the English landscape. For the first time it was lit up at night. If you have lived in the countryside, on moonless nights it is so black you have to feel your way along the roads, along the lanes. We forget this in our well-lit towns. Arkwright lit the mills up at night. The machinery thundered for twenty-four hours a day. The interesting thing is that it attracted attention from the start. Joseph Wright, the great painter of Derby, came out and painted the Cromford Mill at night in 1789. It was a phenomenon, a revolution in itself.

The water-power revolution was relatively short-lived, and with steam power that followed you could place your mills closer to the ports and markets. Yet water power is not quite dead and gone. At Richard Arkwright's Masson Mill, now part of a great complex that began in 1771, some of the water power has actually been harnessed to turbines, which are still capable of producing a third of all the power needed for this giant mill.

So the Derbyshire mills go on, but this valley never suffered from being over-industrialised. Contemporaries would not agree. They regarded the manipulation of the river as the desecration of the natural scene that they knew. Yet now we might regard it as picturesque again in a rural sense. The fisherman sitting here today reflects the older world.

63. Dirtlow Rake, near Castleton: this is one of the most prominent of the old 'rakes' where the lead ore has been picked out by hand over many centuries, certainly since Roman times. The pick marks can clearly be seen. The whole looks like a natural geological formation but is entirely man-made.

96 *Derbyshire: No Stone Unturned*

64. Stone Edge smelter chimney, high up on the moors: it is said to be the oldest standing industrial chimney. Built in the 1770s, it was isolated yet conveniently on the main route to Chesterfield, which had a great trade in lead.

65. Magpie Mine: worked for some centuries, certainly right down to the 1950s, it has now been partly restored as an industrial monument by the Peak Mines Historical Society. Though much lead remains below ground, the deeper levels are flooded and unlikely to be reopened.

66. Cressbrook Mill: built in the style of a country house in the 1770s by Arkwright, and much rebuilt in 1815. Behind the mill is a magnificent mill-pond. The whole valley was manipulated to create this scene. The picturesque valley was stripped of most of its woodland to supply fuel for the new industrial population. The whole site is worth exploring on foot.

67. Near Bonsall, an old mining village, you can still see the small stone-walled fields of the miner-farmers and the scattered barns: a typical dual economy with a marked effect on the local landscape.

68. Curbar Edge: this packhorse bridge was on one of the main routes for lead into Chesterfield market. Though there is an eighteenth-century date on one of the stones, this must represent a later repair. The original bridge is likely to be much older.

69. A broken landscape of former lead-mining: the pattern of shallow pits and miners' coes can be seen most clearly from the air, as here at Bonsall.

70. Yatesoop Sough: one of the many *soughs* which form an intricate pattern underground, many discovered by ardent and courageous local historians of the lead industry. Such soughs were first made in the 1630s and grew larger and larger with experience.

10. Norfolk and Suffolk: Breckland and Broads

East Anglia is a part of England that attracts me enormously, Norfolk especially, and the Broads in particular. As in so many parts of England I cannot help feeling that its fate today may be in the balance: at least as a place where one can find small-scale and human landscapes. Still the Broads are utterly distinctive and refeshing; a watery landscape, slow-moving rivers and large sheets of open water. Only avoid them in the summer.

East Anglia, like the rest of England, is a countryside in which you can find wonderful diversity. Thirty or forty miles from the Broads to the west and stretching over into Suffolk is the Breckland. No two areas could be more vividly contrasted than the Breckland and the Broads. Yet they are separated by no more than the width of Norfolk.

To my eye the Breckland, which means land which has been broken up, by the plough that is, is a desert in everything but its name. We never think of calling any part of England a desert, but the Breckland in fact is the most arid part of Britain. It was made into a desert by the people who first settled here, and nature finished it off. They cut down the original woodland for fuel and building, only to see their light soils blown away by the strong easterly winds. This was a natural disaster, and disasters of this kind, of wind and water, have played their part in the making of the English landscape, overwhelming at times man himself. This arid desolation of the heathlands is relieved by groups of shallow lakes. They lie in gentle-sided valleys, though to look at Foulmere and its surroundings it all seems pretty flat. But a rise or fall of a few feet can change a landscape.

The origin of the Breckland meres is still a little mysterious, although they are almost certainly the work of nature. It could be that they are set in depressions formed ten thousand or so years ago when large masses of ice created a hollow as the ice melted and the water just filled in. The one called Rymer, probably a corruption of Ringmere because it was originally circular, is the meeting point of no fewer than ten parishes. Now, when you get ten distinct parishes converging on one pond, it meant obviously that it was of great value to peasant farming for miles around. It was indeed an English oasis in a dry land, like all the other meres.

The River Lark, though, is on the edge of the Breckland, and that attracted the earliest groups of people moving into this area. Iron and Bronze Age remains have been found all along its banks: it is one of the most fascinating rivers in England from that point of view.

West Stow in Suffolk is one of the most dramatic archaeological discoveries of recent years. It is a very early Saxon village – so early that it overlaps with the Romans. Like a lot of very fine sites it was discovered by chance – in fact it was the planned rubbish dump for a local council, but unlike most local councils who would have hurriedly covered the whole lot up and said nothing about it, this one became interested, called in the professionals, and so we now have a reconstruction by experts of what a very early Saxon village looked like.

The Saxons arrived here in the late fourth century. They overlapped with the Romans for a century or so and they stayed. We still tend to think, because of the way we were taught – and still may be for all I know – that each wave of invaders, Celtic, Roman, Saxon and so on, came in and pushed the others out: all neat and tidy 'periods' one after the other. This is pure nonsense. Over the generations, of course, individual families moved and rebuilt their houses. And each dwelling they abandoned left behind enough evidence to show the archaeologists of today what had gone into the houses and how they were built. A reconstructed hut, carefully done by experts, is the first visual evidence we have of old English society, the very early Saxon period round about the year 400. It shows you the amount of local material which this economy used and had been using over the centuries. There are three different sorts of timber in the hut, and then a filling of daub, which again is purely local – a mixture of clay and sand and straw used to fill in the gaps between the upright timber posts, otherwise it would be a frightful, draughty house, impossible to live in. They were clearly denuding the woodland slowly because this village was a great deal bigger than would appear, probably about seventy house-sites here at one time. Each house used at least twenty fully-grown trees in its construction. And of course each family burnt large quantities of timber to keep warm, and nearly all their implements, big and small, from carts and ploughs downwards, were made of wood. So all in all they must have made an enormous impact on this landscape for the two or three hundred years they were here.

Well, the first village was deserted, not at one go but slowly, thirteen hundred years ago. After that, for some reason we do not understand, medieval farmers took over. We know that because underneath the present soil signs of medieval ploughing have been found – what we call ridge and furrow – and that lasted for centuries. The present site of West Stow, as marked by church and hall, is about three-quarters of a mile to the east of the earliest village. Not a great move, but why? A similar shift took place at Maxey in Northamptonshire, as excavations have shown. It is clear that the history of the English village is much more complicated than we imagine.

Then what with the landscape being slowly denuded, stripped of its woodland cover, and becoming more and more sandy, there came a real catastrophe – a great sandblow such as East Anglia sometimes gets today. This was about 1300, and it buried the medieval fields to a depth of between two and three feet with pure sand. It was largely because of this that the

Stow site has been so well preserved – rather like what you can find in ancient Egypt in dry sand. So the whole landscape again changed completely through a natural catastrophe. Two or three feet of sand just fossilised the whole landscape, or rather buried one and created another.

The sandblows (because there was more than one) that overwhelmed the fields around West Stow must have had a disastrous effect upon the whole of the heathlands. For one reason the Breckland had already attracted a great number of villages. When you come across one of these village sites, and there are nearly thirty in all, you may see just a few humps in a field, and nettles which are always the sign of previous human occupation because they grow where there is a heavy concentration of nitrogen in the soil.

It was the pressure of population that drove the medieval peasants up from the fertile Lark valley on to the remote and arid heaths, but once they got there they too stripped away the natural vegetation – mostly trees – and created, without knowing it, their own dust bowl which in the end brought their farming to an abrupt finish. Yet even in the face of a disaster like that the medieval landowners, the bigger ones anyway, produced a sensible answer, even if the clues that remain for us are obscure.

When the sand overwhelmed the Breckland, turning it literally into a desert, it became a huge rabbit warren, and the various big landlords appropriated areas and called them so-and-so Warren. The Prior of Thetford, for example, took over an area in the very heart of the Breckland. To keep control, like a nineteenth-century gamekeeper, of the local peasantry who poached all the food they could get, he appointed a Warrener who was an officer of the Priory and lived in the Warrener's Lodge – a curious little building – in total isolation. He was liable to be murdered any night by poachers. The lodge was fortified, with tiny windows and a stout door, and he lived on the upper floor for safety. The Thetford Lodge is about the best example of these little fortified houses occupied by the medieval gamekeeper for a monastic house. Rabbits were a valuable crop for a big landowner as well as a nice pie for the local peasantry. So this is the next stage in the evolution of the Breckland landscape.

When one now looks at the surrounding woodland, one can see the slow regeneration of the original Breckland landscape. It had been obliterated centuries ago; it had gone for fuel and building and remained like that because of grazing animals which stopped any young growth. But even as a 'desert' this was a landscape that was still carefully used. A flock of sheep is a rare sight today, but for centuries a shepherd and his flock crossing the heath was a typical Breckland scene. The heath made excellent summer grazing – not enough to support an entire village, but it still had its use. Now, over most of it, all you can see today, apart from the new woodland, is the odd cottage and a solitary church, generally in ruins.

Still, there are places where the diverse landscapes created by our ancestors have survived

– the Norfolk Broads in particular, yet even they have seen great changes. The lower reaches of the River Bure and its tributaries bring you into them unexpectedly. A boat, in fact, and a sailing boat preferably, is the only way to get into most of them. They are well nigh inaccessible, thank goodness, by car or footpath. They occupy only a small piece of Norfolk just to the north and north-east of Norwich – but everybody knows about them, and they are almost entirely devoted to pleasure sailing. Like the Breckland heaths, though, the fate of these beautiful inland waters rests upon a delicate balance of forces. For me, it is the origin of these expanses of water that provides the greatest fascination. This is not just a piece of antiquarian nonsense, because the Broads represent perhaps the most extraordinary manipulation of the natural landscape by our medieval forebears.

When you see a big stretch of water like Hoveton Broad – one of the many Broads in this bit of Norfolk – you cannot imagine it was ever man-made; it looks perfectly natural, not least because there is so much of it, and also the shores are extremely irregular which also makes the whole thing look like the work of nature. It was not until fairly recently that three experts – a geologist, a botanist and a physical geographer – combined to look into the whole problem of the true origin of the Broads. I expect the first man who suggested they were man-made was regarded as a bit of a crackpot, but these three experts proved that he was right. This is a man-made landscape.

The evidence for this staggering idea came chiefly from a number of sources, amongst them the records of the Abbey of St Benet. Now that is a ruin and hardly even that, just traces in the fields beside the River Bure and a surviving wall or two. But the monastic records have survived and they take us back to a time when the monasteries of England were the great capitalists, above all because of their immense ownership of land. Here too there was the continuing problem of the English climate. The coast of Norfolk is bitterly cold; there is often an east wind, and the problem in these parts is to keep warm, even to prevent freezing to death. There is practically no woodland, but the peasantry found at a very early date that they were sitting on the top of masses of peat which, when dug out and dried, could be burnt as fuel. So it starts further back than we know as a purely peasant way of keeping warm in a bitterly cold climate. The peasantry, having started the whole business of using their resources under the ground and around them, then gave ideas to the monasteries – and there were no flies on the monks – that this could be quite a big commercial thing, and at St Benet's, or St Benedict's Priory in the flat land near the River Bure, we have the earliest records of the sale of turves on a big scale. This Priory had acquired the rights of turbary, which really means the right to dig the turves and dry them. That meant, of course, the peasants did it for them, and St Benet's got the rights of turbary in twelve or thirteen different parishes.

When you go down to one of these Broadland parishes today, you find that there is only one place where the peat, in quantity, could have come from – the present-day Broads. We are indeed talking about an industry, a big industry; the removal of nine million cubic feet of peat over the centuries, and the creation of hollows and pits approximately four square miles in area. Even the natural-looking edges of the Broads could be explained away. Boring showed that the steep margins, which had collapsed or become overgrown, could only in the first place have been made with spade-like implements. Indeed, there are still straight-cut sides in some places. In Barton Broad, it has been established botanically that several balks of peat which still stretch out into the Broad were composed of the original uncut peat. They had served as causeways between two sets of diggings. Elsewhere similar balks were found which were parish boundaries, which is why they survive. You did not obliterate such ancient things as property boundaries.

Still another question remains: how did the medieval peat-diggers cope with what must have been a continual seepage of water into their pits? Possibly by simple baling-out to start with. Before the 1300s the sea, which is not very far away, was in fact twelve or so feet lower in relation to the land than it is today. As a result the peat diggings did not fill up until there was this really big change in relative land and sea levels in the thirteenth century. Suddenly large areas of the pits flooded to a depth of several feet and so made what we now call the Broads.

The records of St Benet's tell us that the monastery, and all the land around it, was flooded in a great 'sea surge' in December 1287. The Chronicler adds the graphic detail that the water rose more than a foot above the high altar in the abbey.

The Broads still cover thousands of acres but they are in fact diminishing quite noticeably in size. At Hoveton we know from an old map it used to be 130 acres but in the course of the last 140 years, which is not a long time in terms of nature, Hoveton Broad has now diminished to 76 acres. It is almost halved in area of water. What is happening is that the woodland and plant life of all kinds, large and small, is being regenerated very quickly, and in parts it is almost like an Amazonian jungle. In some places it is at the mud stage but nature is obviously taking over again, and seedling trees are establishing themselves.

Nature never stops work; trees and scrub have grown up along the River Bure, over-whelming the acres of reed, rushes or sedge there used to be, which had been in their time such marvellous natural products with all sorts of uses. Our ancestors wasted nothing. Even a great disaster like the sea surges, the sandblows, the Black Death – even after all these both man and nature recovered and passed on the old inheritance to us. Perhaps it is something we are learning to do today, though I suspect we shall not learn the lesson in time. My worst fears are confirmed whenever I find some sensible ancient craft or skill coming to an end. The reed cutter, for example, is the last to follow his craft. Nobody will follow him, yet he is part and parcel of the English landscape. His is the human hand which tended it, making it unique, something different. The kind of peasant who created the old world.

It is the distinctiveness of East Anglia that brings me back here time and time again. In fact I have even gone as far as to say that Norfolk draws me like a woman. Well, born in Devon, perhaps my mind is accustomed to a different topography and here I can see the landscape with a completely fresh eye. When I go to Norfolk, as I do too little for my liking, I know when I have crossed the invisible boundary. The skies change, the landscape reflects a different light, the special light that illuminates the whole county and helps to create in itself a unique landscape.

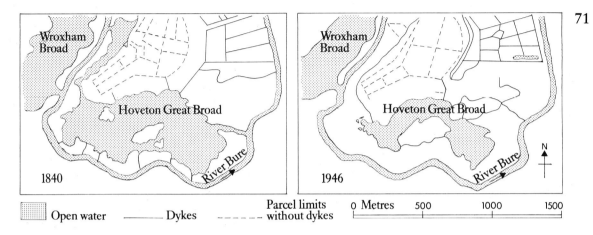

71. Hoveton Broad: the shrinkage of the Broad proper, due largely to the fact that it is cut off from the river Bure, is clearly revealed by this comparison of the Great Broad as it is shown in the tithe map of 1840 and the wet area as it lay in the year 1946. The whole area, with the now Great and Little Broads, shows almost every stage in the process of regeneration, from silt which is not disturbed by any flow of water and so attracts what may be called primary vegetation, to the almost wooded areas which make a distant view look like an untamed Amazonian forest on a miniature scale.

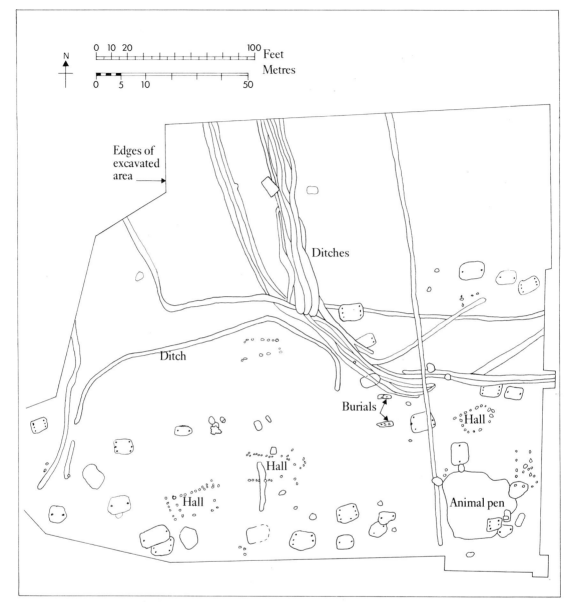

72. West Stow: the site of the ancient village of West Stow lies a few miles north-west of Bury St Edmunds and a mile or so west of the present West Stow church, on the edge of Forestry Commission plantations. The site, on a five-acre sandy knoll beside the River Lark, has been completely excavated and revealed a long series of settlements; the plan shows only the Anglo-Saxon village, its houses, rubbish pits and ditches. The site was discovered in the late 1940s but not excavated until 1965–72. The once-fertile area had been buried by a great sandblow *c.* 1300 AD: thus the site was remarkably well preserved. The Anglo-Saxon 'village' had some eighty buildings consisting of single-roomed houses in groups around larger 'halls'. The date of the earliest houses is very early, *c.* 400 AD, overlapping the end of

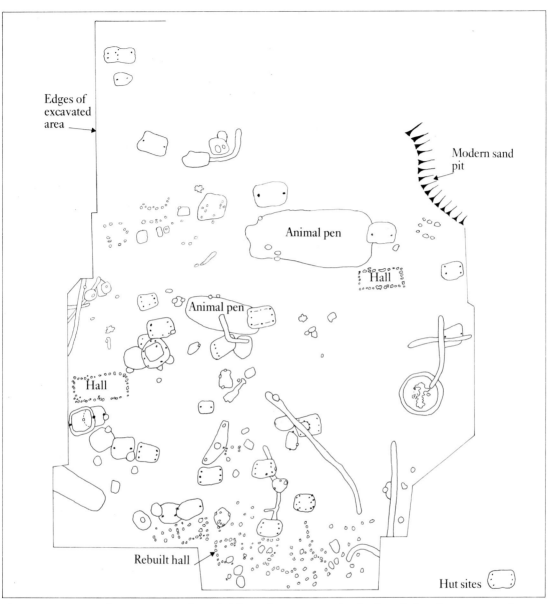

Edges of
excavated
area

Modern sand
pit

Animal pen

Hall

Animal pen

Hall

Rebuilt hall

Hut sites

the Roman period, suggesting the initial settlement was invited and that for a generation or so the two peoples lived side by side. By 650 the site was abandoned, for reasons that are not yet clear, and another site chosen a mile or more to the east.

The whole site is very complex, as the plan shows, for here is encapsulated the history and development, over two and a half centuries, of one of the earliest 'English' villages. The excavation is now complete, the work of analysing the results well under way, while new ideas about Anglo-Saxon buildings are tried out by reconstructions of some of the houses and a hall on the original sites. The intention is that the reconstructions should form a piece of 'living history' as a focal point to a Country Park.

110   *Norfolk and Suffolk: Breckland and Broads*

73. Hoveton Broad in the background, cut off from the river Bure and so slowly being recolonised by vegetation. Salhouse Broad in the foreground.

74. This, which looks totally unlike any of the Broads, is what is happening on the edges of Hoveton Broad as there is no river-current to keep the silt and mud on the move. The density of the advancing vegetation is remarkable, and the Broad is only about half its size two or three generations ago.

75. West Stow in the heart of the Breckland. This early Saxon village, which overlapped with the Roman settlement in the Lark valley, was overwhelmed by great sandblows and buried and rediscovered by accident. There were sufficient remains of the earliest huts to reconstruct the scene, following an expert excavation.

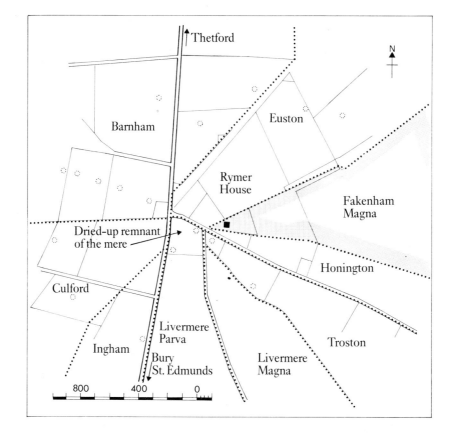

76. The arid wastes of the Breckland are, fortunately, dotted with shallow *meres*, ponds of water which lie in what were glacial depressions in the landscape. As water was so scarce, it was carefully allocated to various parishes. Rymer ('ring mere' from its old shape), shown here as a dried-up remnant, became the meeting-place for no fewer than nine parishes, all of which had access to the water's edge. Such an arrangement of parish boundaries is a sure indication of some lost archaeological feature of great significance.

77. Barton Broad on the river Ant in Norfolk: the peninsulas and lines of reed-swamp patches mark the submerged balks of peat, many of which were preserved from digging because they were historic parish boundaries.

78. The Breckland: a typical view in this, the most arid part of Britain. Farmed since neolithic times, but obliterated by sandblows (the greatest about 1300) with thirty buried villages. Vegetation is creeping back over the sand, and the Forestry Commission has taken over huge areas for its trees. The Scots pines, standing high above the rest, are again a typical scene in these arid parts.

79. Warren Lodge in the Breckland: now on Forestry Commission land but really in the heart of the Breckland. Looking strangely like an isolated medieval castle, it was in fact a fortified Lodge for the warrener who looked after the rabbit warrens that were a valuable source of profit to the medieval monastery. No one who did not know the strange history of the Breckland could possibly guess what its origin and purpose really were.

11. Northumberland: The Making of a Frontier

Northumberland, a land of far horizons, where the clouds themselves pile up like mountains, or drift mistily along the rounded hills, above all the Cheviots, the boldest of them all. A wild landscape, but marked all the same by two thousand years of man's hand, and up here in the mists the Scots and the English drew their boundary. But it was not settled at a stroke by any means; in fact it was the result of centuries of fighting, first one side coming in, then the other side sweeping through the hills, with vengeance in their hearts and weapons in their hands. So this border country belies its peaceful appearance today. Beneath its clouds are the scars of centuries of warfare and skirmishing.

Before England and Scotland came into existence as names, the Romans were the first to divide the island of Britain into two. Hadrian's Wall, which everybody has heard of, runs across the neck of England from the Tyne to Solway Firth. It is no longer a frontier, since it bisects the county of Northumberland, but it was the first effective division, and once it was there the stage was being set for a prolonged and bloody series of attempts to finalise the division between what we now call England and Scotland.

Hadrian's Wall is still very impressive, following to the horizon the line of the rock called Whin Sill – a natural escarpment of hard rock that was the obvious choice for the Roman builders and defenders. But what a posting 'the Wall' must have been for these men from the Mediterranean! In this damp and windy climate, 'Posted to the Wall' must have sounded the end to those men, like being sent to the Russian front in the last war. And after the Romans left Britain in the early fifth century, it was to the north of the Wall where the problem of the frontier line was to be fought over for almost 800 years: first of all between the emerging kingdoms of Northumbria and the Picts and the Scots, and then later between the established nations of England and Scotland.

It is only on the top of the Cheviots – a natural watershed – that you get a visible barrier between the rival kingdoms. But even here the summits are mostly rounded and generally lack a well-defined peak – so not surprisingly this remained disputed land for a long time. For most of the time, though, this disputed country was occupied and fought over by people who were not in the least interested in England or Scotland as names or nations. This was great cattle country, and the farmers on both sides were more interested in pasture than politics, and in doing whatever was necessary to survive – stealing, killing and burning.

It is very hard to believe that this huge, empty countryside was once overpopulated, but so it was. Back in the sixteenth century, and even before that probably, the custom was for a man to divide his property at death equally between all his sons. The result was that nobody got quite enough to live off. At the same time it was such lovely country they could not bear to leave it, so the younger sons, at least, took to stealing cattle as a way of life. Now cattle-stealing as an occupation has gone, and what we are left with – since the farms were too small anyway – is rarely a farm in sight, no people in sight, only the cattle and the sheep.

What took place in these now peaceful hills was just like an early version of the Wild West. Most of the fighting was about the stealing of cattle and horses, with the Scots more often raiding us than we raiding them. That is not just simple patriotism – it is because England was a richer country, with more to be looted. So, across this kind of hilly no-man's-land, families and clans fought it out. And as if this lawlessness was not enough, from the thirteenth to the sixteenth centuries especially, there was always the threat of outright national wars between the Scots and the English.

In this long struggle, Northumbria was the key place of attack and danger. When the Scots flogged the English, in the notable victory at Bannockburn in 1314, it must have put the fear of God into everybody in this part of the country, including the greatest magnates of this area, the Percys, the Earls of Lancaster and others. They felt the need, even if they had castles, to strengthen them enormously. At Warkworth, you find one of the finest examples of all. It is a huge place: it was begun by the Normans, then the Percys acquired it, and soon after there came the traumatic experience of the Battle of Bannockburn, the fear that the Scots were on the doorstep, as indeed they were at Berwick. So the Percys enlarged the Norman castle into the splendid fortress whose ruins we see today. Most of what we can now see is the work of the Percys in the early 1300s. It is the direct result of the Battle of Bannockburn and the increased fear of what the Scots could do.

The fear of the Scots produced in the Northumbrian landscape an extraordinary number of impressive castles. Bamburgh, with a wonderful profile that is almost too good to be true, built on a headland that offers a naturally defensive site. Even Holy Island had its own castle, built on a volcanic outcrop. And above all there is Dunstanburgh, built in the early years of the fourteenth century by Thomas, Earl of Lancaster, for himself – the fortress of a very rich man, and also his home in a really violent time. Everyone, though, besides the rich men, needed some protection, so there are scores of other fortified dwellings in Northumberland, and they can all be fitted into some kind of social order.

There is a remarkable little farmer's house, high up in the real frontier country at Gatehouse, before it had ever been demarcated – within a mile or two of the Scots. It is an old bastle house, sixteenth-century I suppose, built next to the real farmhouse, with entrances for the cattle down below and steps for the household to get to the upper part. So it was family up above, cattle down below. The door was obviously barred with a heavy oaken bar which made them more or less secure, but it was terribly isolated. If help came they were lucky; otherwise the corn would be burnt, the cattle stolen.

At Embleton, beside the parish church, you got a quite different kind of fortified house. It belonged to the vicar, and it is a type called the Vicar's Pele. Only the rich vicars could afford this kind of thing. In the event of a raid, the vicar and his servants and family did a quick move into the fortified house, which incidentally goes back to about 1400 in date, and is a lovely example of its type. Here they not only hid, but defended themselves. It is a battlemented building, with arrow slits, a mini-fortress, and if you could last out for a couple of hours, either the village came to the rescue, or else the Scots moved off.

Embleton is only twenty-odd miles from the misty Cheviots beyond which the Scots could retreat as quickly as they came in. But we must not run away with the impression that the Scots were doing all the raiding. Both sides were as active as each other. English raiders went deep into Scotland. Hermitage Castle, on the Scottish side, the one-time home of the keeper of Liddesdale, is, as a result, one of the most impressive specimens of castle building of the fourteenth century. Originally it was a small hermitage for monks, then it became a castle for the defence of the border. In the fifteenth century it was the bastion of the bloodiest valley in Britain which, even by medieval standards, possessed a brutal and archaic society. 'The Castle of Hermitage,' writes Sir Walter Scott, 'unable to support the load of iniquity which has long been accumulating within its walls, is supposed to have partly sunk beneath the ground; and its ruins are still regarded by the peasants with peculiar aversion and horror.' Well, Hermitage, despite its peaceful name, is the essence of the border land-scape. It still looks as if it might possibly pour forth a troop of border raiders, with their leather jackets, steel caps, and faces set hard southwards towards the hills that defended England.

The constant raiding reached a climax in the sixteenth century and since it was hard enough in any circumstances for any community to survive, let alone grow and prosper, any town that did was remarkable indeed. Most remarkable of all is Berwick-upon-Tweed. This is a real frontier town and hence its magnificent fortifications. It is not only one of the best fortified towns in Britain, perhaps *the* best, but perhaps in Northern Europe also. The reason is the unusual nature of its fortifications, which were an Italian invention. Basically it has bastions that projected from the face of the town wall; cannon were placed in the bastions to fire parallel with the wall – crossfire – so nobody could attack the wall straight on. The whole system is still preserved. As the small people and the bigger people were fortifying their houses and their castles, a town like this, in a really critical point on the coastal plain, changed hands no fewer than thirteen times. Eventually in 1482 it was considered to be English, but still a separate power in treaty-making.

Started in 1555, the fortifications were finished under Elizabeth I, and as a result Berwick never again changed hands. Thus one end of this long frontier was fixed. Elsewhere, even in the depths of the hills, there was some kind of agreed system of government, at the local level at least, for the benefit of the big land-owning families who had got most to lose – the Homes on the Scottish side, the Dacres, the Percys and so on, on the English side, and this meant that stretches of the frontier were slowly being agreed and determined bit by bit. A trout stream could, perhaps, be swapped for a piece of upland pasture, although the feudal lords of this region were more interested in, and measured their wealth by, the numbers of men they could summon to arms rather than any particular features of the countryside.

Windy Gyle is a part of the Scottish frontier over 2000 feet up. It is particularly interesting because the frontier took so long to establish, yet this piece, a few miles long, had apparently already been agreed upon. It was a meeting place for the governing body, the marcher lords on the English side, and their equivalents on the Scottish side. The actual frontier is not far from here – it is marked by something called Lord Russell's Cairn, because he represented the English case, if you can call it that. He was accidentally killed by a Scot, and his name was given to the Cairn which is absolutely on the dividing line. In fact the Cairn is a prehistoric burial mound, and so are several others up here, so here you have another piece of the frontier being established by much older landmarks. It was agreed piecemeal. Windy Gyle had been established by 1586, when the marcher lords met up here.

Elsewhere, though, there are many turns in the present frontier which we cannot explain, except by assuming, as I do, that the great families on both sides, who must have met from time to time, negotiated, and eventually agreed on a line which meant something to them at the time. It was to their mutual advantage to settle disputed territories. The fighting went on, right into the 1590s, between the Scots and the English, some of it official wars, mostly unofficial raids, killing and stealing.

Then suddenly it all came to an end. The crowns of England and Scotland were united in 1603. The age of war finished, and the age of peace began. At Belsay you see it dramatically. It had its effect very quickly on the architecture in the landscape, and in the landscape itself. You see a great fortified house and, built right up against it, a house in what would have been then the modern country-house style, Jacobean, 1614, built within ten years, or almost ten years, of the Union of the Crowns. These people were so confident that peace had come that they could build a house in this way. The transition between the two ages is shown visually in really quite a small detail, the narrow slitted windows of the fortified house of about 1400, contrasted with the big windows of a Tudor or a Jacobean country house. For the first time they could have these large windows and look out upon a peaceful countryside, indeed look out on their own parkland. For the first time they felt safe.

Even on the limitless moors, the new peace left its mark. The sheep could safely graze. In winter of course the moors were unusable, under deep snow, but by the spring, the new grass was coming, and the sheep were moved up from the lowland farms, up to the spring and summer pastures. All over the moors you have a special kind of building, the shielings and the stells, words peculiar to the North Country. The shieling was the little building where the shepherd lived for about half the year, lonely but safe. Stell is a Norse word, meaning stall or pound. They are nearly always circular, built of stone, and used when the shepherd wanted to round up the sheep for clipping or for some other purpose.

To get the cattle and sheep away from this region to the distant markets, a number of tracks were used that still traverse this now empty countryside. Some of them may even be prehistoric in origin. Many of them, like Clennel Street, climb over the hills from the Scottish pastures into Northumberland as if the frontier did not exist. For centuries these ancient border tracks were used by Scottish drovers to bring their cattle down to be sold in the nearest of the English markets, where Scots cattle were always the favourites. The Union of the Crowns of England and Scotland saw a revival of the old drove roads. In their heyday, the eighteenth century, it was said that a hundred thousand cattle travelled these trackways each year over the mountains.

Many of these tracks come down into the Northumbrian dales and eventually converge, and when they do, we find that rarity of this empty landscape, the village with its own characteristic frontier features.

For me, the village of Elsdon sums up the border. Everything is here: a splendid vicar's pele, an enormous village green, and of course inns for the drovers. It has one of the best village greens in the north of England. It is very big, because it is so near the Scottish frontier. The Scots would come sweeping down over the hills, and this big green served two purposes. One was in a time of trouble: you drove all your cattle into the green, and then stockaded the gaps between the houses – that brought the village cattle in to safety. On the other hand, in times of peace, it was also a small market town, mainly dealing with cattle. The men of Tynedale selling cattle and buying cattle, and the men of Reedsdale, when they were not actually stealing each other's cattle, legitimately dealing in a market. The green was in fact the grassy market place. On the edge of the green is a stone cattle pound – and beyond it, in the middle of the green, possibly for reasons of security, is the parish church. It is a very nice example of a frontier village, however peaceful it may look today.

Now the frontier is completely defined, even to the bold sign put up by British Rail, as trains thunder by from Edinburgh to London and back again. At the end the frontier drops into the sea, and the sea falls upon it all with a meditative indifference. It reminds me of the marvellous words of James Ogilvie, one of the great Scottish lords, when he put his name to the Articles of Agreement for the Union with England. He put his pen down and said, 'Now there's ane end of ane old song.' Eight hundred years of strife had ended.

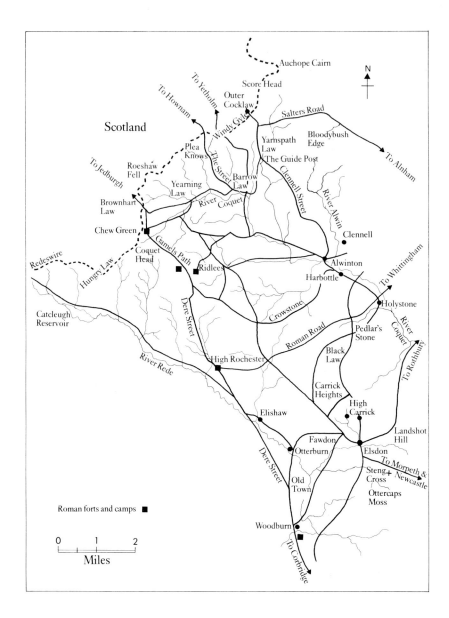

80. The drove-roads of the Anglo-Scottish border: there are no true passes through the Cheviots but here and there a convergence of tracks shows where it was possible to drive the Scottish cattle over the top down into the fattening pastures of England. Many of these 'roads' have their own names, such as Clennell Street, Gamel's Path, and so on. These tracks can only be traversed on foot, though an intrepid driver in a Land Ranger could just about manage the climb. Having crossed the Cheviots the cattle-drovers tended to aim for nodal villages such as Alwinton and Elsdon, where large greens accommodated them and their herds at night.

81. Clennell Street: one of the many drove-roads over the top of the Cheviots, by which in times of peace the Scottish drovers drove their cattle from the lean pastures of Scotland into the fattening pastures of England and ultimately to the great cattle markets of the English Midlands. There were few passes over the high Cheviots. The 'roads' converged on these and thence diverged in various directions. Some are still (just) passable roads, most are deep scourings on the steep hillsides.

82. Belsay Castle: showing the transition from war to peace on the Anglo–Scottish border. The fortified house was built in the turbulent fourteenth century, and the house behind added in 1614 with the Union of the Crowns.

83. All over the Cheviots and their foothills are circular stone structures like this, known as stells (from the Norse word for a stall), where sheep could be rounded up off the hills for shearing, or getting to market.

84. Black Midden: one of the finest of the surviving 'bastle' houses along the Border. This was the fortified dwelling of a yeoman farmer, equivalent to the rich man's castle along the coast. Probably sixteenth-century, a time of particularly bitter fighting in these lonely hills.

85. The walls of the Border town of Berwick, mostly Elizabethan in date. The town changed hands many times between Scots and English as the key on the coastal plain. It is still one of the most spectacular fortified towns in Europe, certainly in Britain.

86. Dunstanburgh Castle: one of the most romantic ruins along the Northumbrian coast, greatly strengthened from 1315 onwards, the year after the decisive Scottish victory at Bannockburn.

126   *Northumberland: The Making of a Frontier*

87. Hermitage Castle: the most impressive castle on the Scottish side of the Cheviots. Near here a religious recluse had his hermitage – hence the name of the castle, which was certainly completed before 1244. There were many such Scottish castles, but this is the finest remaining example.

88. Elsdon: a frontier village on the Northumbrian side of the Cheviots, with its large green that served as a cattle market in times of peace and as a refuge when the Scots were raiding over the hills. The vicar's pele, or fortified tower, is one of the finest in this turbulent countryside.

89. The great cattle pastures of the Cheviot Hills, coveted and fought over by both English and Scots, and for centuries disputed territory.

12. Devon: Land of my Fathers

I had the good fortune to be born in a part of England which had suffered very little change over many generations, in a small and ancient city with unravished country all around it. As boys we could reach the fields within ten minutes' walk in any direction. Holidays we usually spent only ten miles from home in the deep peace of inland Devon.

There was no village where we stayed. It was a landscape of small farms and cottages and a small manor house where the squire's ancestors had lived, so I was told by my country cousins, since the time of Alfred the Great. The present head of the house is the descendant of a long line of Devonshire squires, John Fursdon. I know now that his family have actually lived here since the time of Henry III without a break, and that takes us back nearly 800 years, possibly further if we only knew. They take their name from 'the furze-clad hill' – that is what Fursdon means – behind the house. Fursdon of Fursdon. There are quite a few of these ancient families left in Devon who take their surnames from the place where they began, and over the many centuries they have made their own intensely local landscapes. At Fursdon the furze has gone long ago with the improved farming, but the family name and the family go on.

The Devon landscape has all my life brought me face to face with some fascinating and often puzzling problems of landscape history. At the age of seventy, it still does. I look at it with the same enquiring eye. This is where I really became interested in why certain things are as they are. Devon is a mixture of more or less isolated single farmsteads, and of hamlets, which are usually three or four farmsteads grouped together. You rarely find fully-blown villages as you do in other parts of England, and the real problem is this: what does this countryside of isolated farmsteads really mean? Have they always been isolated? I do not know all the answers, although over the years I have traced the history of enough of these farms, not only in documents but by walking the fields and the lanes, to be quite satisfied now that they have always been like that. Isolated in their lonely little valleys, beside a glancing stream.

Chilton is a perfect example of an isolated farmstead. It always has been isolated, never part of any bigger place. We know it belonged, as part of his royal estate, to Alfred the Great. In his will, made about AD 880, he left this farm and a lot of other land to a younger son: 'Child's Farm', it means literally, but Child has a special meaning – the son of a noble or royal family. So it belonged to Alfred in those days. I think it is even older than that, but no matter.

What still fascinates me is that when I was a youngster, my country cousins who lived round here used to stuff me with the yarn – so I thought then – that it had all belonged to Alfred the Great. Now they could not have known this as an historical fact. It was not written down anywhere. So I think it is either a very long oral tradition in the countryside, or else perhaps Alfred the Great was a kind of father figure in these parts and was a reality even in my childhood in the 1920s. Another farm which goes back to the time of Alfred and before is Coombe Barton, at the end of a narrow, winding lane. It is a good farm, successfully and continuously farmed for over a thousand years, chiefly because the first farmer here made the perfect choice of site.

There is a marvellous little spring at Coombe Barton, coming straight out of the rock. It is the fountain and origin of life at this spot. If it were not for this spring there would be no big farm here. Coombe Barton is still isolated. It has depended all through its long history on this water supply. There was a farm here in the seventh century, thirteen hundred years ago, and it is also mentioned by name in the Domesday Book of 1086. The water supply has never failed, not even in the great drought we had two years ago. And it is fresh water – none of your polluted chlorinated stuff.

Even in these communities of isolated farms you nearly always get a parish church. But what happens if there is no obvious centre like a village? How did they decide where to put the parish church to serve such a scattered countryside? The answer is not always obvious. Some churches were built on prehistoric sites which had been of pre-Christian religious significance: the best example that I know in Devon is Brent Tor, on the edge of Dartmoor, 1130 feet up in a bitter climate. Now why should anybody build a church so that you had to toil up this volcanic tor for every christening, marriage and funeral? And as for funerals, the amount of soil at the top is so little, that you wonder if they could have had any burial there at all. They did in fact. They could have chosen anywhere else in the parish for their church, but they chose what appears to be the most difficult place of all. But I am certain about Brent Tor's origin, that the Christians took over a place of pre-Christian worship: indeed, around the base of the tor is a man-made rampart that dates from pagan times.

A lot of other churches are sited where they are because they were founded by the local landowner, who might have had quite a small estate. A good example of this is a very small church called Honeychurch, which actually lives up to its lovely name. The place-name experts say it gets its name from bees making honey in the tower. This is complete rubbish. It is the church of one Huna: it is 'Huna's church'. He was an Anglo-Saxon landlord who founded the first church next door to his house for his own convenience. He wasn't going to walk a mile to any church, the parishioners could do that. It is a place that is soaked with many centuries of Latin mass spoken to a small gathering of Devonshire farmers and labourers and their households. Everything about it is leaning and old: the woodwork, the benches, are fifteenth-century. You may think that Devonshire rustics listening to a Latin mass sounds incredible. But when, in 1549, Parliament enacted that the Mass should be read in English it led to the biggest Catholic rebellion in Devon. The natives, rustic as they were, resented the changeover from Latin to English and weeks of bloody fighting followed.

Most of Devon has been cattle and sheep country from time immemorial. As a pastoral farmer you did not need any capital equipment. You just settled down near a stream, out of reach of any flood water of course, but all you needed was your water supply, and a few rudimentary farm buildings. Around the occasional village, in contrast to the isolated farm, we see more arable land where in the past you simply had to co-operate with your neighbours to work thousands of acres in open fields, and also to share the heavy capital cost of plough-teams of eight oxen.

Most arable farms in Devon are found on the famous redlands which are a startling red, sometimes blood red, especially when you see them in winter just after ploughing. And they have a particular origin. I do not mean just geographically. They are very fertile. They still fetch the highest prices when they come into the market, and they were the great prize of the Anglo-Saxon Conquest in this part of England. Sweeping in, in the mid-seventh century, from the east and the north-east, the Anglo-Saxons acquired the whole of the redlands of Devon as a prize, and pushed out the native Celtic farmers already there, pushed them up into the pastoral hill country.

You may wonder why there are villages in Devon at all. Thorverton is a particularly good and very nice one and a special part of it called the Bury gives us a clue about its origin. The native farmers were chucked out in the Anglo-Saxon Conquest, pushed up into the hills, and Thorverton and places like it were military plantations. This explains its shape. Its original shape is simply a kind of stockade, a very wide rectangle, in case of trouble from the natives. To this day it is called the Bury, which is a slight corruption of an old Saxon word, *Burh*, meaning a fortified enclosure: it is still a big rectangle which could house all the cattle while the crisis lasted. It has been partly built over in modern times, but basically it is a stockade type of plan. There they were living in a potentially hostile countryside though I doubt if there was much fighting at all. Every harvest, in past centuries, was a great gamble. It could fail. You could die of hunger, so you did not waste time fighting about the land, you got on with the job of farming. One of the other essential things of course for any settlement, especially a big village, is a constant water supply, and here at Thorverton there seems to be an absolutely endless spring. In all my life I have never seen it fail.

As we see it today the English landscape is a product of centuries of human endeavour. But there were failures as well as successes. Lydford appears to be just another one-street village now. It started life in the rather wild country round the very edge of Dartmoor as part of King Alfred's chain of fortresses against the Danes in the ninth century. It seems a bit improbable that the Danes should ever come so far inland as this, but they did. Alfred created four fortresses in Devon, of which Lydford was one, so it had a purely military origin. It is also very interesting because it was apparently planned from the start as a town with a grid-iron street pattern. But the side streets off the long main street never got built up. The 'planned town' is older than we ever thought.

Lydford quietly died and you can detect the signs to this day. You get a kind of crossroads of two green lanes crossing the main street: in fact you reach rock bottom in a way. Not just a failed town, but two failed streets. Why such a complete failure? After the Norman Conquest two much more important castles were built, not many miles away, so Lydford lost all its military importance. And again the facts of geography were against it. It is on the edge of Dartmoor: it had no hinterland, as the geographers say. 50,000 acres of the parish are spread across this awful countryside and there simply was not the population or the produce to support even a little town, though we know it had a licensed market, and even its own mint for a time.

There is another link between Dartmoor and Lydford, not of special landscape significance, but it is a bit of English history that still stands firm. Lydford Castle looks like a perfect little Norman castle. In fact it is not a castle but a prison, and it was built for that purpose, but for a special kind of prisoner, those who offended against the forest laws of Dartmoor or who offended against the so-called laws of the tinners, the laws of the stannary. So it has survived as an almost perfect specimen of twelfth-century building, and it had one great moment in its history. We do not know about most of the people who were thrown in the dungeon here, but one man we do know about. Richard Strode MP had criticised the tinners in the House of Commons for the way they polluted the rivers with their waste. When he came down this way they grabbed him and threw him into the dungeon. As a result of the subsequent row over treating an MP like this, the decision was made that whatever was said in the House of Commons was absolutely privileged, as it still is. It was the Strode case in the early 1500s that settled that constitutional point for good.

Devon actually had some seventy boroughs in medieval times, but about a half of them failed to survive, especially those around the edge of Dartmoor. Many a decrepit-looking village in Devon was once a medieval borough. Some are little backwoods villages like South Tawton, but even that, in the twelfth century, spawned the nearby settlement of South Zeal on what was then the main road from London to Land's End – the old A30.

South Zeal is first recorded as a name in 1167, when the road had attracted perhaps an inn, a smithy, and a few houses from the mother village. By 1299, there must have been enough growth at South Zeal to encourage the lord of South Tawton to get a grant of a weekly market. It was a hopeful speculation. The widening of the street where the chapel now stands represents the old medieval market place, and yet it all failed, not enough trade came their way.

In striking contrast to all the failures, some places succeeded beyond question. Most important of all, Exeter, my native city. With about a hundred thousand people today, it started as a village 2000 years ago and it could not fail, and here and there scattered about it are little enclaves that have escaped the eye of the planner and the engineer. (I put the road-engineer as a worse menace than the planner in my own mind.) Little courtyards, medieval almshouses, even a medieval spring: it is still at heart a small city. You can walk around it, in spite of all the destruction, and see things like the original twelfth-century bridge which was being built at the same time that London Bridge was being rebuilt in stone, and you can still see considerable lengths of the original Roman walls built about AD 200. And, I need hardly add, the cathedral, which has for me the most harmonious interior in England – not the most impressive, but the most harmonious of them all. It is the Mother Church of this lovely countryside and on Christmas Eve it is crowded from end to end.

Well, not all of Exeter is that ancient. The house where I live is late Georgian in style. Exeter expanded rapidly in the 1830s and 1840s, a middle-class refuge for the elderly of independent means: but within ten yards of where I live there is a lane, a built-up road now, which is Saxon in origin. It is still called a lane and it runs for about a couple of hundred yards and joins the Roman road that connects Exeter with its port at Topsham. So even here there is a Saxon road and a Roman road not far away.

Exeter – this is the centre of it really – to me, anyway, has had to change but it goes on. To me it is indestructible. The Germans tried to finish it off in May 1942, and they gloated the next morning – 'Exeter was a jewel, we have destroyed it'. They did not succeed, though they did terrible damage: but since then the city council, to my mind, has nearly finished the job off. Not quite – there are some things that could not be destroyed – the cathedral, the city walls, and so on: it is a place that will be living on for another two thousand years as it has up to now.

I was born here, my family have lived here for a hundred and fifty years, and I can quote the tag of Horace: 'Hic amor, haec patria est' . . . 'This is my love, this is my country'. In short, this is where I belong. This is my own landscape.

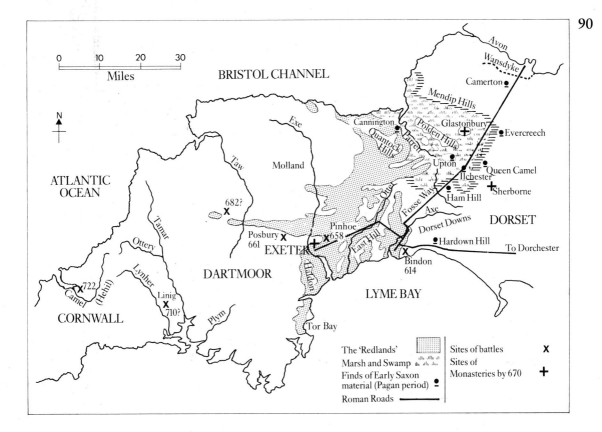

90. The 'red lands' of Devon, rich soils that derive from the New Red Sandstones and were the great prize of the Saxon Conquest from the early seventh century. The whole of these fertile lands passed straight into royal hands and most remained so down to the Norman Conquest and after. Much was also granted away by various kings to abbeys like Exeter Abbey *c.*670, now represented by the cathedral.

91. Honeychurch: to the left is the site of the former demesne farm of the Anglo-Saxon lord of the manor (Huna) who founded the original church, probably in the tenth century, close to his own house. Hence 'Huna's church', probably built of wood and rebuilt by the Norman lord of the manor *c.*1150 in stone.

92. Isolated farms in mid-Devon, in the parish of Cadbury. There is no village, only some twenty isolated farms scattered about the landscape from the beginning. All were there before the Norman Conquest.

93. Most of the ancient hedgebanks have been destroyed by modern farm machinery, but many original hedgebanks survive, dating back a thousand years and often more. The older banks are usually massive, partly overgrown, and almost impenetrable. This particular lane, formed by a double hedgebank, is known to date from about 670 when the King gave land to Exeter Abbey.

94. Exeter was founded upon a hill rising a hundred feet above the river, probably more than two thousand years ago. The cathedral rides along the top of the ridge – dominating the old city before modern subtopian expansion. In the foreground is the Exeter Ship Canal, the oldest ship canal in the country, now disused except for pleasure.

95

96

Devon: Land of my Fathers

95. Lydford: now a dull single-street village (except for the ancient parish church and the twelfth-century castle not in the view) Lydford was founded, above a steep-sided gorge for defensive purposes against the Danes, by King Alfred in the late ninth century. It seems to have been planned on a grid-iron plan from the beginning, but many of the side-streets either never got built up or decayed centuries ago.

96. Lydford: this narrow, grass-grown lane, running at right-angles off the surviving main street, represents one of the side-streets which never got built up. Lydford was primarily a military foundation and though it had a mint for a short time (from *c.*980 to 1066) and a market, most of the side-streets remain mainly grassy tracks.

97. South Tawton, with a typical conjunction for Devon of the parish church and the fine medieval 'church-house', probably built about 1480. Such church-houses survive in considerable numbers in the remoter parts of Devon and served primarily as what we should call parish halls in places where there was no real village centre. Parish feasts were held in the hall on the upper floor, while the ground floor was used chiefly for storage.

98. Morwellham on the Tamar: once a busy port for shipping copper and tin from the mines up in the hills. The harbour, which reached its peak in the middle decades of the nineteenth century, had decayed by about 1900 when the richest copper mine closed down – the famous Devon Great Consols. But a great deal remains to be seen, and the site is now a very unusual and lively museum.

99. Most of the Devon churches were rebuilt in the fifteenth century and early sixteenth. Broadclyst church is a particularly fine example of this period.

100. Brent Tor. The parish church is built on the summit of a volcanic outcrop some 1130 feet above sea-level. It is first recorded *c.*1140 and was known as St Michael of the Rock. Because of its extraordinary position there can be little doubt that it took over a pre-Christian site, regardless of the total inconvenience for medieval villagers.

Index of Place Names

National Grid four-figure references in brackets

Bold numbers refer to illustration pages